August Schemmel

How to make money out of inventions

August Schemmel

How to make money out of inventions

ISBN/EAN: 9783744736862

Printed in Europe, USA, Canada, Australia, Japan

Cover: Foto ©Lupo / pixelio.de

More available books at **www.hansebooks.com**

HOW TO MAKE MONEY

OUT OF

INVENTIONS,

—AN—

ADVISER FOR PATENTEES,

—BY—

AUGUST SCHEMMEL.

• • •

NASHVILLE, TENN.
CHAS. LeROI, PRINTER, N. CHERRY ST.
1890.

INDEX.

PLEASE READ.

As generally the introduction is not read, I put the above caption over mine. So far as I am aware, no author has ever tried to write a help and guide to inventors, though every inventor must acknowledge that such a guide is necessary. The position of most inventors, I find after long observation, to be the following :

In a lucky moment the invention was born. With hard toil of perhaps months and years the inventor worked at the product of his mind before it was finished. Full of hope, he has at length completed it, and waits for the granting of his patent. That happy moment comes. He has his patent. Yes, but what now ? He must make the patent profitable, and that is often very difficult. Sometimes all trials are unavailing, and why ? Because he did not introduce it himself. It is a well known fact that no one can speak as well for a thing as the inventor himself. No one can explain all the uses and value of an invention as he can. It is therefore not advisable to trust to a stranger anything that can be done by the inventor.

To help and advise inventors I have printed this book. In it will be found all that is necessary for the realization of an invention : The names of thousands of firms, which will be of use for the selling of patents ; brokers, if one wants to sell stocks ; newspapers, for advertisements ; and contract formulas. In fact the inventor can find in it every thing that is necessary to enable him to help himself. Wherever I could I have given examples, so as to make it more clear, and also to make the reading matter as interesting and attractive as possible, and to show what this or that inventor was capable of doing.

✳ Part ⁜ First. ✳

CHAPTER I.

USEFUL AND INTERESTING.

IT is an old truth, that the ability to invent and the capacity to turn the invention into money, is very seldom united in one head—just as scholarship and philosophy rarely stand together. Though an inventor must have technical knowledge, in most cases, still his mind takes a different turn from that of a merchant and seller. While the eye of the inventor looks thoughtfully on the problem of his mind, the merchant looks in the distance. On account of this difference it is easily explained why the merchant's view of an invention is quite different from that of the inventor. The merchant regards the invention as he would any other salable article, though he too can be mistaken in its value; but the inventor sees his invention only through the eyes of a lover, or as a mother would her child, or an author his book. To this physiological discord, in regard to the value of the invention, others are added from the circle of criticizers, which help to tangle up the opinion. Even the locomotive, steamboat, and the sewing machine had much skepticism to conquer.

We must excuse if many inventors meet us with a great deal of self-consciousness. The world has sinned much more through its unbelief than inventors have by their over-estimation. The goal of the inventor is generally the making of money, so he always tries to sell or use his patent in the most advantageous way.

The needs of inventors, whom study or accident gave a lucky idea, are vastly different. Not every invention can be used, and not every idea is an invention. How many old ideas are thought about as new, and how many people are working on a "perpetuum mobile" yet? "Not every ignorant man is a dunce," Seume says, and so it happens that many a learned head tries problems which will never bring him any good. Any help which prevents the throwing away of money, time and wisdom is therefore a great boon.

One could ask, when will the period come when nothing more can be invented, when everything is so good that no improvement is necessary? To this I will answer, that as soon as a land stops to make progress it is going backward. Inventions arise out of the discoveries of wisdom. As this always shows the material in new and different lights, so inventions help to give us new uses for them. The development of inquiry for many necessities, is the attraction to find out something new and better. Even the labor question has supported the progress of invention; especially the United States have shown that high wages aid the advance of machine work, and, through this, have a good effect on industry. The area of inventions and the development of them is so great that the human mind has, and always will, find something new. It is a good sign of our culture that industrial advance must not always be paid with the martyrdom of the person, but that it often helps him up to a fortune and social standing. Inventors stand on a level with statesmen and scholars, and those who inherit wealth and title; for the good derived from inventions, and the energy and sharpness of mind which is bestowed on them is not behind science or statesmanship.

That one can earn money, and sometimes a great deal of it, through inventions is only the acquirement of the last century. The ancient records do not tell how much this or that celebrated philosopher, poet or artist earned. The middle ages, also, do not record much of the private life and financial standing of inventors. Under the progress and intercourse of city life, and the influence of geographical and scientific discoveries, industry makes advances which the ancients never thought of. Art enriched itself with oil-painting and the many engravings; strategy with new weapons and ways of transport; house-furnishers with beautiful fire-places, expensive carpets and articles of luxury out of glass, delfware and metals. Goldsmiths wrought, with wonderful patience, things which will even now create envy. The most valuable thing on earth, time, was obliged to submit to a more complete control through watches and clocks. Human thought was penned up in the insignificant little signs which typography called into life.

The middle ages record more of the life and earnings of painters, sculptors, architects and alchemists than of inventors. Any way, the inventors could not make money until the state granted them a right of possession. Such a right was first issued in the sixteenth century, by a state which was very anxious to advance in industry. In England the first patent was granted in 1623, though, of course, this was a very simple thing, called a privilege, and was granted to the inventor for a certain number of years. In the year 1791 the first was granted in France. Germany had introduced patents already in the beginning of the century, but each little state had its own way of granting them, and therefore in no land was the invention protected as little as in Germany. In July, 1877, there first appeared a united German patent law.

This is not the place to make war against the betrayer of invention rights, and still less to carry it on in the one-sided way that is generally the case. It has no, or very little value to defend or assail the invention right without regarding its relation to other rights. Though the patent right is very incomplete, still it is better than none. Without a patent no invention can bring money to the inventor. A great hindrance to the introduction of new inventions is the "practical man." By this I do not mean the man who works in his special field until he masters it; he has theoretical knowledge enough, if not to invent new things, still to accept what others invent. This is the real practical man, and he can only be praised. But the practical man, as one generally understands, is one who knows all about his article, but nothing else. His look only goes as far as the old; he will not acknowledge the newest improvements; even the greatest new invention he only calls plan-making. When he finds that an invention is really useful, he will sulkily accept it, so as not to be too far behind the others. But never would he give his money and time for things that the whole world had not already found good. It is this practical man, as I have said before, who is a hindrance to improvements. For years he kept back the use of smelting oven-gases, and it is his fault that now so much of this gas is allowed to escape. It was such a man who, when the optical telegraph was invented, said, " Do not use this manner of correspondence. I am a practical man, and I believe that the best way is to sit down, write a letter, give it to a messenger and put this man on a horse." In the next generation his follower would say of the telegraph with its unseen power for transmitting sound: "I do not believe in your unseen power. I am a practical man, and believe only in the optical telegraph, which I can see working." Just so the practical man acted when they showed him the Siemens regenerator oven. "Nonsense," he said, "you turn coals to gas and then burn them again? I am a practical man, and when I want heat I light my coals and burn them." No better did he think of the Bessemer steel. The behavior of the practical man has also the following reason: If anybody comes to him with improvements and offers them to him, it offends him, and he cannot understand how a stranger, and a man perhaps younger than he, who, it may be, does not understand every thing of the branch which he wants to improve, can make any inventions in it.

Sometimes the owners of large establishments are technical men, but generally they only think of the selling part. In such cases the decision falls to the lot of the headman, who is often, for some reason or other, a practical man.

Of course, it is true that more than one-half of the patents are useless; still the advance of the nation is dependent on them. The army and the navy, the whole strength of the nation depends on the restless, eager inventors. Many inventions are suppressed through the efforts of the practical man. Think of Bessemer! Long years he worked in vain. The practical man laughed at him, and put many hindrances before him, but he won. Did Watt, Stephenson or Faraday have any better lot?

Many professional inventors ought to be suppressed, but still it is always better to endure them than to act like the practical man, who watches another build a house without helping him in the least, and, when it is finished, is ready to move in, and even like the cuckoo, crowd out the rightful owner and live in it alone.

The inventors, hurt because the money and the people do not run after them, very often because they do not know how to use their patent profitably, especially if it is a foreign one, permit their self-assurance to sink slowly to the freezing point. They forget when they have to bring their patent to the market, and that the taxes are not paid, so little by little the patent becomes void, and leaves the owner nothing but the knowledge that he once possessed patents. Often it is the inventor's fault, who, after giving much money toward making the patent, does not give enough to advertise it. He thinks that millions of people have been waiting for his patent, and will receive it gladly and pay thousands for it.

The value of an invention lies not always in its real worth or the wisdom and energy of its inventor, though this is nearly always the case. Luck plays an important part, but I will not say that it always helps those who are forsaken by Minerva.

To lay an invention before the eyes of the world and keep it there, one needs a firm will and a firm belief in the thing itself. The plain idea of an invention can arise out of many reasons, and is not always the principal thing; it can be the result of hard study or of an accident.

Now and then an original mind strikes a new vein and gives the inventive human a mighty impulse which lasts through centuries Most of the inventions are not entirely new, but only modifications and improvements of old ideas known to very few and not in public use. When we read the story of mechanic inventions, we often see a new idea which suddenly vanishes and is not heard of any more until some one, on account of the needs of his time, commences it anew and following the footprints of the others, makes it successful. There are inventions which are invented before their time, these are projects which, because there are not means enough to complete them, must wait until they are needed. This explains why many inventors now can do what their predecessors were unable to do. Louis Napoleon says the following on this subject: "Inventions which are ahead of their time must remain unused until the common intelligence rises up to them.."

The circumstance that most inventions are products of the past is used by a kind of socialistic law to put down the fame of inventors and even to try to assail the patent rights. Of the first part of this attack, which assails the fame of an inventor, Reuleaux, the famous author of the Kinematic, remarks: "When I would try to show how new machines and new mechanisms are built, I do not intend to put down the value of inventions in the machine field. I only would find for the inventive head new and valuable means to work. I want to raise the ideas, not to put them down. Only one who has not invented old things, that is, spent much time on a subject and then found that some other person had made that before, can look down on inventors that have done this. Often they say it is the inventor's fault, but it is very easy to do this."

The ownership right of inventors has as just a claim as all the other rights. Some one can accidently discover a mine, and yet the law gives him sole right to it.

The right of patent ownership is the simplest among its fellows. The proud right of the land owner is first, and is followed by the simpler of the capitalists, the mine owners, the authors, the artists, and last of the whole row the much abused, limited, highly taxed inventors It plays the role that philosophy has under the sciences, according to Kant. Though the queen of them all, it carries the light for others.

What an invention is, and especially a new invention, people never agree about. As before mentioned, there are very few entirely new ideas, which no man has thought about, and which would sink the words of Ben Akiba, "There is nothing new under the sun," into the ground.

The writings of gone centuries have in them thoughts and ideas which are very much like ours. For instance, in the works of the learned monk, Bacon, we find these interesting remarks : "I will point out some of the wonders of beautiful nature, which are no magic art, and which no magic art could produce. There may be instruments made with whose help one man can make a ship sail faster than those filled with sailors. One may make a wagon which will ride with unbelievable fastness without horses or any other animal in front of it. And flying machines will be constructed in which a man can sit comfortably and fly above in the air like a bird. A little machine will be invented with whose help a man can pull thousands of his fellow-creatures even against their will, to himself. Also, machines with whose help man will be enabled to descend into the depths of the ocean without danger."

This one extract shows us that our forefathers had just as many ideas and just as good ones as we, and that it would be very hard to say and prove that any idea we now have is absolutely new. Between an idea of an invention and an invention itself is a great step. By some inventions the central point is the idea, in others the practical development of it. For instance, after the treatment of vulcanization and hardening of India rubber was invented, out of these few inventions ever so many others were made ; the India rubber was used as water-tight material, elastic beds, and many other things ; almost in every business it is needed. It is made into jewelry, stamps, billiard balls, and pressed articles of many kinds. In short, the ideas were here the principal things, and not the technical difficulties.

We are satisfied with saying that all things are new inventions if they are a good deal different from any thing of the same kind already invented. Accordingly, if the difference is large we call it a new invention ; if smaller, an improvement or an enlargement. As soon as the first sewing machine was made this idea was not new any more; perhaps even before Howe had made his first model, others had thought that an iron tailor would be very good, and, may be, some had tried to make one, without success. Notwithstanding, hundreds of sewing machines were patented, for each one had a little originality.

Who, in our time, has any special work and does not try to know at least a little about the improvements and new inventions in his branch, must be a very strange man. However, just the inventors are very little inclined to compare their ideas with other people's, and study about their branch. Often the inventor is not even very well acquainted with the profession he wishes to reform. Arkwright had, for instance, no idea of textile industry, and only his firm will to complete his invention, helped him through the many difficulties and made him a rich man in the end. Leblanc, the founder of the soda industry, was a doctor ; Paxton, whom we must thank for the first world's fair building, was a gardner ; Armstrong, inventor of the cannon of the same name, was a lawyer ; and so we could give many other examples in almost every branch of industry. It is a plain and well known fact, that the men who invented the greatest military improvements were peaceable citizens and not soldiers as we might suppose. Just as little as engineers invented powder, guncotton, or dynamite; it was not they who contrived the torpedo, the field telegraph, and many other things so essential to our modern strategy. All these inventions came from private technologists. All these things must be regarded, if one has to judge inventions of amateurs. If there is a little doubt on the part of professionals, still they should always bear the above mentioned facts in mind.

The examination of an invention to find out whether it is new or not must be treated in various ways, if you want to find out in foreign lands or in your own country. For when an invention is found new in one country and is protected through a patent, this may not be the case in other countries, and what is really new in one may be long invented in another, or even obsolete. It is astonishing, sometimes, how long it takes for a thing that is really useful, to find its way from one country to another. Before the sewing machine came into use in Europe, eight years had passed, and while England and America used steam-engines, it took long for the continent to follow.

It is not always the great inventions that bring riches; no, quite simple, common things of daily use. Even more or less useless things can make a pretty good profit if they are patented. During the world's fair in Philadelphia an American named Cooke had a so-called continental fan, in the shape of an American eagle, patented and sold the fan at five cents a piece, selling 700,000 fans, and making considerable profit. Great inventions do not always pay immediately. Bessemer used up many thousands of dollars before he got even a penny out of it, and if he had then lost patience and stopped putting money in he would have lost all.

As the inventing and trying of a patent is the technologist's part, so the selling and making into money is the merchant's. In short, after a man has invented something he must turn into a speculative merchant to sell it. To give rules for the sale of a patent is very hard and nearly impossible. Examples of how others use theirs is the best way to find out. Therefore, in another chapter I have mentioned some. In most cases, however, the talent and luck of the person must help.

Not always, nay, scarcely ever, has the patent holder money enough to build a factory for his article himself. Very often he has to ask for help to be able to patent it. The way to find out who will lend money, is to advertise in the newspapers. In many cases active partners are not necessary, and one finds often private gentlemen, widows with some capital, and clerks, the most willing to assist in the manufacture of a good article, and by it increase their property. These, of course, are also the people who are cheated out of their little money by swindlers, because they are simple and believe easily. The story of great sensational patents and inventions is often a swindle. I know a case of a man who, with the help of a refusal of the patent office, of which he showed only the upper half, succeeded in making a good natured banker lend him fifteen hundred dollars ; another inventor of this kind entrapped a harmless restaurant keeper and swindled him out of sixteen hundred dollars. Every good idea may be misused, and we mention the above for the good of patent holders and inventors, to show them that it is not always an active man who will lend them money.

At the end we will say what good patents do for some classes. In what degree they are useful among working men, one can read out of the report of an English manufacturer. He tells first, that though he possesses many patents, he never invented anything, but that he bought them all. Poor men and working people were those whom he bought patents from. In his whole neighborhood he knew of no employer who had invented anything. Once he went into a poor hut and there found a man working on a machine which was fastened to a wooden chair, the only one in the house. This machine was patented and he himself was the owner of the patent.

CHAPTER II.

WHAT IS A PATENT?

With the name " Patent," " Erfindungs-Privilegium, (invention privilege,)" " Brevet s. g. d. g., (sans garantie du gouvernement, without guarantee of the government,)" one designates the received permission to manufacture a newly invented article, or to make anything with a new process, during a certain number of years, in a certain country. The receiving of such a privilege and the holding of it during the longest time is dependent on the fulfillment of certain things.

These patent laws fall into two groups, one the application and the other the examination.

The application used in Belgium, England, France, Italy, Luxemburg, Norway, Austria, Portugal, Sweden, and Spain, does not give the patent holder the least guarantee that his patent is new. It simply consists: that with the addition of a patent taxes receipt, description, and perhaps drawings and model, the inventor presents to the magistrate a petition to grant or give a patent to the invention described. If this petition and the description, drawings, etc., are written and sent in a formally correct style the patent will be granted, without an examination to find out whether it is new or not ; it being supposed that it is new. If, now, after some time, perhaps, it is found that the invention was not new it gets void and is lost. The examination, at present only used in America, Canada, Denmark, Germany and Russia, is not only in regard to the formally right application, but also to the newness of the invention, and in America, Canada and Russia it even regards the usefulness.

But not even this examination can give a positive guarantee, for even the patent officers may overlook something, and the patented invention may not be new. Any way it gives a greater security and certainty of the validity of the patent than an unexamined one. The invalid declaration of a patent can occur during any time between the granting of the patent and its expiration, and may happen because it is not new, or because the inventor carelessly forgot to pay the dues. In most cases there must be a third person who hands in the declaration and gives the evidence.

CHAPTER III.

WHO CAN RECEIVE A PATENT.

WE must distinguish—

a Invention patents.

b Introduction patents.

c Improvement patents.

d Addition patents.

a Under invention patents, to distinguish them from introduction patents, one understands the first privilege to manufacture an article in any country. This is granted without caring what nationality the applicant is, whether a foreigner or a citizen of America, Belgium, Canada, Germany, England, France, Italy, Austria, Portugal, Russia, Sweden or Spain, but only to the original inventor, or his descendants and substitutes.

In Luxemburg, only to a native inventor.

If a man who is not authorized has applied for and received a patent, the real owner and inventor can dispute with him for the patent.

In Denmark and Norway, the one who mentions or applies first to the magistrate.

b Introduction patents are those which are patented in foreign countries, and are now sought for in this country, therefore are applied for after the first patent is gained. These can be applied for and received by any one who is first, excepting in America, Canada and Sweden, where they are only given to the foreign inventor or his descendants, and in Austria, only the foreign patent holder or lawful descendants can get it.

c Improvement patents are patents on improvements of already patented inventions, without hindering the rights of a third, and everybody can receive them. In Russia, however, during the length of the original patent, only the holder can get an improvement patent. In some other states a certain time is reserved for the holder of the principal patent, during the limits of which he alone can get a patent on an improvement of his article. In France, one year; in Italy, six months; in Portugal, one year.

d Addition patents are improvement patents which in Belgium, Germany, France, Italy and Spain, are granted as additions to already existing patents. These only the holder of the original patent can receive. They are not subject to yearly taxes.

CHAPTER IV.

WHEN MUST FOREIGN PATENTS BE APPLIED FOR?

In France.—Before the invention is anywhere described through prints, or is in any way published so that any expert third can make it.

In Spain.—Invention patent for 20 years.—As the above, with the further rule that the invention must not be patented in any other country before the application.

In Spain.—Invention patent for 10 years.—At the latest, within two years after a patent has been granted in another country.

In Belgium.
In Denmark.
In Germany.
In Italy.
In Luxemburg. For invention patents.
In Norway. Before the invention has come into use in any country, or is anywhere described through prints or is published so as to enable an expert third to make it.
In Sweden.
In Portugal.
In Russia.

In England.
In Austria.
} Before the invention is manufactured by a third, or brought to sale, or if it is so described as to enable an expert third to make it.

In Canada.—Within a year after it is patented in another country.

In Portugal.
In Russia.
In Spain.
} For introduction patents

Before the invention is manufactured or used in the country.

I would especially advise the patentee to be very careful in applying for patents in foreign countries. Only apply for them in a certain order, to make them last as long as possible.

CHAPTER V.

HOW LONG DO PATENTS LAST?

*In America . . . . 17 years.
*In Belgium . . . . 20 "
*In Canada . . . . 15 "
In Denmark . . . . 5–10 "
In Denmark, introduction patents, . 5 "
In Germany . . . . 15 "
*In England . . . . 14 "
*In France . . . . 15 "
*In Italy . . . . 15 "
*In Luxemburg . . . . 15 "
In Norway . . . . 5–10 "
*In Austria . . . . 15 "
In Portugal . . . . 15 "
In Portugal, introduction patents . . 5 "
In Russia . . . . 3–10 "
In Russia, introduction patents . . 1–6 "
*In Sweden . . . . 3–15 "
In Spain . . . . 20 "
In Spain . . . . 10 "
In Spain, introduction patents . . 5 "

Introduction patents become void in the countries marked thus * at the same time with the first invalid and first applied for foreign patent; in all states where nothing is mentioned they last as long as invention patents.

Addition patents never last longer than their original or invention patent.

CHAPTER VI.

OF GREAT IMPORTANCE TO OWNERS OF FOREIGN PATENTS.

In the patent laws of all foreign countries, with the exception of Germany's, is a paragraph which says that if a patent, through any circumstance whatever, should become void, the patent in this land will also expire; in other words, if in Belgium, for instance, the owner forgets to pay the tax or neglects anything and the patent is lost, he will also lose it in all other countries, with, of course, the exception of Germany. The principal reason that so many patents are lost is because the owner forgets to pay the yearly tax. We therefore mention all the countries where it is exacted:

1. Belgium, 10 francs, and for every following year 10 francs more; that is, for the second year 20 francs, third year 30 francs, etc.

2. Germany, for the first and second years, 50 marks, and then for the other years, an advance of 50 marks per year, making 100 marks for the third, 150 marks for the fourth year, etc.

3. France, 100 francs every year.

4. Italy, for the first year, 50 lires, for the 2–3d years, 50 lires; for the 4th–6th years, 75 lires; for the 7th–9th years, 100 lires; for the 10th–12th years, 125 lires; for the 13th–15th years, 145 lires.

5. Austria, for each of the first five years, 26.25 florins; for the 6th year, 39.37 florins; for the 7th year, 46 florins; for the 8th year, 52.50 florins; for the 9th year, 59 florins; for the 10th year, 65.63 florins; for the 11th year, 78.75 florins; for the 12th year, 91.87 florins; for the 13th year, 105 florins; for the 14th year, 118.13 florins; for the 15th year, 131.25 florins

6. Russia, for the first year, 90 rubles; for the 2d year, 120 rubles; for the 3d year, 180 rubles; for the 4th year, 240 rubles; for the 5th year, 300 rubles; for the 6th year, 360 rubles.

7. Spain, for the first year, 100 pesetas, and for each following year, an advance of 10 pesetas per year.

Furthermore, a correct patent can be lost through the following reasons:

A special examination to find out whether the article is new or not takes place in very few countries. This examination, and the patent afterwards received, does not guarantee that the patent is absolutely new and valid to its end. Everybody in this country, as well as in those where no examination takes place, has the right to insist on its annulment if he thinks it is not new, and if he can prove it old it is annulled.

In England a patent which has several new points gets void if one of the points was old when the patent was applied for.

If an inventor and patent-holder expects such a writ of error, they can meet it with a disclaimer before it has been presented at court.

In England and France it is lost if the invention proves to be useless.

If the patent is not renewed in time in Canada, England, Italy, Luxemburg, Austria and Portugal it is lost.

It is lost if the inventor has not manufactured the article in the given times, as follows:

Belgium, within 1 year after the manufacture in another country.

Canada,	within 2	years after receiving the patent.			
Denmark,	" 1	"	"	"	"
Germany,	" 3	"	"	"	"
France,	" 2	"	"	"	"
Italy,	" 1	"	"	"	"

If the patent is of shorter duration than six years.

Italy, within 2 years after receiving the patent if it last six years and longer.

Luxemburg,	within 2	years after receiving patent.			
Norway,	" 2	"	"	"	"
Austria,	" 1	"	"	"	"

Portugal, within the first half of the duration of the patent, for invention patents.

Portugal, within 1 year after receiving the patent, for introduction patent.

Russia, within the first quarter of the duration of the patent.

Sweden,	within 2	years after receiving the patent.			
Spain,	" 2	"	"	"	"

In France and Canada, if the patent-holder and

his partners import the article into those countries, or if it is imported with their knowledge.

In Germany, if the state buys it for use in the army, fleet or for the public welfare, and in Portugal, if it is useful to the public.

———◆———

CHAPTER VII.

———

WHEN IS AN INVENTOR ALLOWED TO MANUFACTURE AND SELL AN AR-TICLE FOR WHICH PATENT HAS BEEN APPLIED?

———

In all countries, with the exception of Denmark and Norway, as soon as he has sent all the manu-scripts, drawings, etc., which refer to the invention to be patented, and are necessary to the attainment of a patent, also the tax which is required, to the magistrate.

In Denmark and Norway from the first day the patent is issued.

CHAPTER VIII.

THE VALUE OF A PATENT.

It is very natural that every patentee thinks his patent will make him a millionaire. Many believe that some rich man has been waiting to offer him the money for the patent. A gentleman said he had invented a new electrical apparatus, and asked $300,-000 for the patent, and he would not even give evidence whether the apparatus was good or not. He thinks it is self-evident that *his* patent is the most useful in every way. Of course, nobody would give such an enormous price, and the consequence was that the patent was never manufactured, and in six months another man had invented something very much like it, and as he understood the business better, made lots of money. Much the same fate Dela Bastie had with the German glass manufacturers. He thought his hard glass method for Germany was worth ten million francs, and he asked one million for his invention. The result was that he was very artfully cheated out of his invention, and made little money with it in Germany. Such examples I could give by hundreds, and prove that through too much self-assurance and overrating the patent holder destroys his patent. This is very hard to keep from overrating, for there are certain loose patent agents who tell the inventor that his patent will sell for any large sum, in order to get money out of him

To name a certain sum and say it is the value of a patent, is nearly impossible, as has often been proved, and the inventor can be certain that at the highest he gets only one-twentieth part of the value of his invention, and often only one-fiftieth of its value is offered him. If this strange circumstance is examined, it is generally found that it is the fault of a certain unbelief on the part of the buyer. For even with the best patent, he can never be sure whether he will lose or gain by buying it. This insecurity drives away most purchasers. If the patent is very enticing, it may find many who want to buy it, but the price is lowered a good deal on account of the distrust.

The first thing that is of great importance to the buyer is the manufacturing cost. If great sums are needful for this, it will make it very hard for the patent to be sold, as a view of great manufacturing costs always puts down the value of an invention. If this point is decided to the satisfaction of the buyer, his next thought is whether the article needs many advertisements or even traveling men. If it does, the price is again diminished, and so perhaps the inventor receives $500 for it, while the buyer makes a profit of $100,000. But what is a patent of this kind worth which the buyer pays $500 for and makes $100,000? I think that if the inventor would get 20 per cent. of this, making $20,000, it is not too much. I am sure that my honored readers will agree with me, and some, perhaps, say that the inventor ought to get still more. Still one must also think of the large capital which the buyer was obliged to use in order to make the patent profitable.

That inventors may not have bad luck, I would like to give them a system which I think is the most reliable, and most likely to give them a durable and good income out of their inventions. First, only let the patent for a certain royalty, and in the first year for a small one, perhaps 10 to 20 per cent. of the selling price of the article. In the second year, 20 to 25 per cent. of the selling price, etc. Besides, the buyer has to pay the inventor all the expenses of the patent, etc. From all these revenues the value of the patent comes all by itself.

CHAPTER IX.

THE KIND OF INVENTIONS THAT FIND GOOD SALE IN FOREIGN COUNTRIES.

ENGLAND—Machines of every kind, firing methods, transport ways of every kind, telegraph, steam cars, electricity, cotton industry, and others.

France—All the above mentioned, and besides notions, gloves, dress articles, shoes, artificial flowers, advertisement wagons, fancy articles, etc.

Italy may be regarded more as an agricultural than an industrial state. Of the patents granted in Italy, from 40 to 50 out of every 100 are from foreigners. Though there are patents of every kind, agricultural implements and mill works predominate, also articles for vineyards, wagons for wheat, baking ovens, and similar things are numerous, while all inventions that indicate higher culture are absent. Stoves for the heating of houses are not to be found, though they are quite necessary, and under the rubric "steam cars," we find more inventions for the cooling of the cars than for the warming.

Russia—Inventions in regard to the size of the territory are very good, for instance improvements of steam cars and telegraphs, in the beet sugar line, the manipulating and making into soap of fats, agricultural implements, musical instruments, etc., bring good profits generally.

In Germany and Austria all good and useful United States inventions are easily sold, and at good profits.

Sweden and Norway are, for metallurgical processes, firing and wood-stuff manufactures, very recommendable.

Denmark is very advisable for nautical improvements, as well as advances in agriculture, raising of stock, and fishing.

CHAPTER X.

DIFFERENT POSSIBILITIES TO MAKE MONEY OUT OF PATENTS.

THE possibilities to make money out of patents are various, and mostly depend on the kind of patent. We have,

1. The selling of the patent for a special at one time payable selling price, to one or more persons or to a company. The buyer gets all rights and profits without any further sum.

2. The selling of a patent for a small sum (which in reality is but to cover the expenses of the patent and all that belongs to it and is regarded as such) and a royalty. This is also to one or more persons or a company.

3. The selling only for royalty to one or more persons or a company.

4. The selling of patent rights for some state, county or city, for a certain sum.

5. The selling of the patent right for certain cities, counties or states, on payment of a small sum and royalty.

6. Renting of the patent rights for certain cities, counties or states, for only a royalty.

7. One makes a certain number of the patent article and rents them. This is best done with machines which manufacture the whole or part of an article. So, for instance, the McKay sole sewing-machine was rented out to shoe factories, which had to pay a royalty for every pair of shoes sewed on the machine. The control was easy ; the owners giving the shoemakers stamps which they had to paste on every pair of shoes before they left the factory. In England they had a different method, having in each machine a dial which recorded the number of soles made, and the manufacturer had to pay a certain sum for every thousand. In Germany they hired it for a certain yearly rent. Later on they were sold for good prices, and now about 20,000 of them are in use.

From the above it will be seen how many different ways there are. It is always a very advisable way to sell or rent the patent for a royalty for every piece sold. It is easy to keep control with stamps which the inventor has made and which he sells, for the royalty to the buyer. For machines it is advisable to have little plates made with the stamp of the inventor, and to have these fastened on some part of the machine. To realize foreign patents the best way is to go, after having made good models and descriptions, to the land where you want to interest people. Of course, a knowledge of the language is very important, or an interpreter is necessary. In many cases one can correspond, but only for the contract making it is necessary to travel to the place. What can be done the following case clearly shows : Two inventors packed up a locomotive and brick machine and traveled to Germany where they even had not a patent. After a few days they had sold it for $5600. Another example, which shows that it is best not to insist on a fixed price: A Frenchman had invented a new alligation of metals; he had a patent in France, and before he even had the patent in Germany, sent some one there who was to sell it for $6000. Many would-be-buyers came. The alligation was tried and found good, but all were not anxious to pay $6000. The Frenchman then said, "I do not care to have a royalty per pound on an interest. I want $6000 and not less." But nobody came to buy it. Never persist on a fixed sum if you are anxious to sell. I advise all inventors to take what they can get and not to persist on a sum which is too high.

To realize patents which are only improvements of others, and which are invented by one not of that branch, it is not advisable to handle the patent yourself. The best way is to rent the patent to large manufactories and ask a certain royalty. If this is done a pretty profit can be realized.

CHAPTER XI.

IF AN INVENTOR WOULD SELL HIS PATENT WHAT MUST HE THINK OF MOST?

WHEN he would like to sell his patent he must first make a model of it, that he can prove the invention is all he says it is, or all it ought to be. The inventor must not forget that any one whom he wants to interest in his invention is naturally a little mistrusting and that he needs evidence to assure him. An invention can look real nice on paper and be in reality very useless, therefore a model is very necessary. The next and nearly as important is an accurate and precise description, in which all the advantages and uses of the patent must be especially mentioned. The inventor cannot use enough care on this and the model, as they generally prompt the person to say yes or no. Only have no half models, no incomplete, half finished things, if it is possible, because the same thing can get an entirely different look if it is badly presented. All people look at such inventions quite differently from the inventor. Of course there are things of which no model can be made, which only exist on paper. In such cases it is best to interest people who can make arrangements for the introduction, and who understand the article. If the inventor would act correctly, he must allow them to use his system free, for they introduce it and deserve a great deal. Let us think of the introduction of the sewing-machine into England. Nobody wanted to buy it, as it was very expensive at first. Not until many had been given away did it begin to flourish. "All beginnings are hard." This sentence is very correct if one talks of the introduction of new inventions. I would like to press the inventors to be very modest in their expectations at the beginning, so that they may find people who will take their invention to manufacture, introduce and bring to the market. When the patent is introduced the inventor can raise the royalty and ask a sum 20 to 50 times as high as at first. Those inventors who believe the whole world will run to them are greatly mistaken. When, at the beginning of 1870, Solway, the inventor of the soda-ammonia process, came to Frankfort-on-the-Main and invited the soda manufacturers to come and see him and he would explain it all to them, not one came, and he had believed they would think it a great honor.

Professor Morse, the inventor of the telegraph of the same name, tells us that when he was in Washington to see if he could not induce the government to have the telegraph line from Washington to Baltimore equipped with his patent, he had placed his instruments on both sides of the capitol to show the members of Congress how they worked. As he talked he saw that some, but very few, believed and liked his machines, but more looked at him distrustfully, while others even thought him a swindler. It was toward the end of the session and about 400 bills had to pass before his, so he went home with but fifty cents in his pocket, having spent all on the instruments. He had a very sleepless night, but next morning found that his bill had passed, and a new era founded in telegraph inventions.

CHAPTER XII.

HOW THE PATENTEE CAN FIND A PURCHASER.

(1) He must get himself copies of his patent from the Patent Office in Washington. (20 copies for $2.00.)

(2) He must, if possible, make a model, perhaps smaller than the original, for even that shows the working and shape of the machine better than a drawing. But if a model is impossible, a good drawing which shows the whole of the invention must be made.

(3) The inventor must write an accurate description of the patent and all its uses and advantages, so that a buyer can see them without trouble.

(4) The inventor has to choose, out of the list of firms in the second part, those who can use his patent, and make his offer to them. Here I will warn the inventor again. Never, if a buyer comes, chase him away by persisting on a fixed price. Always be modest. Further, it is advisable not to sell smaller rights than state rights, and not to give them for royalty; for if city or county rights are given, the inventor has thousands of troubles to silence and will be continually at law.

CHAPTER XIII.

HOW MUCH PER CENT. IS THE AVERAGE ROYALTY?

The royalty that a manufacturer has to pay the patent holder or inventor for the manufacture is between 5 and 10 per cent. of the selling price. The per cent. is always in regard to the article manufactured. If it is a small thing and has to be made cheap, the per cent is smaller; in this case the quantity must bring the money. If it is an article which has a large selling price and no competition to be feared, 15 per cent can easily be charged; even 20 per cent. has been given, but that is very seldom. It is for the interest of the patent holder not to ask too high a royalty, for he then, through that, compels the manufacturer to raise the selling price and that may hinder the selling a great deal.

How large a royalty can be asked is best seen by referring to the case of Bessemer, inventor of the Bessemer steel. He received from England and the United States a royalty of a few cents per pound of steel, made by his process, and his income was more than a million yearly.

CHAPTER XIV.

TO FIND A PARTNER.

I have often heard that when patentees seek money they say, "I will take a partner." I have also noticed that it is easy to find one, but I have seen that at the end the partnership was very often not as nice as it promised to be at the beginning. The cause of this we mostly find is the reason, that the partner, though he furnished the money, had no business talent, or did not care to attend to the business. Another cause is the unfriendliness of the partner to the patentee. The partners often think that their money is everything and they forget that the patent is the main part; for without a patent no partner.

The patentees generally look for a partner with much capital, though he may have little business talent, while they would do better with one who had more talent and less capital. My experience has taught me that patentees have very little business talent, therefore they need a good and talented business partner.

In making agreements with a partner, I would advise the patentee to be careful and see that in case of a separation, the patents and inventions should always fall back to the patentee and without any special compensation. Should the partner not agree to this, but want a payment, it is best to fix a sum in the agreement.

The best way to find a partner is to advertise in a newspaper; in large cities, also by going to agents.

The portion which the patentee can ask in partnership is between one fourth and one half of the profit; generally one third. In contracts where the partner receives a certain per cent. on his capital, before the profit is divided, the patentee always receives one half.

CHAPTER XV.

TO BORROW MONEY.

The patentee can borrow money easily from a bank or banker, if he is a well known business man. Besides this, the patentee can have money from private people if he mortages his patent, or gives any other security. As the easiest way to find such private persons, I advise newspaper advertisements. Newspapers for this purpose are in the second part of this book. Besides this, he should offer higher per cents than usual, and should mention this in his advertisements. It is also advisable to offer the lender a small portion of the profits, thus making him a silent partner, which is very recommendable. If the patentee acts according to this plan, he will easily see all his wishes gratified.

CHAPTER XVI.

THE FOUNDING OF A STOCK COMPANY AND THE SELLING OF STOCKS.

If a larger capital is required for the manufacture of a patent, it is always best to found a stock company. For the foundation of a stock company the patentee unites himself with some gentlemen, thus forming a corporation, which must be entered in the state according to the law. The expenses of this act are very small. A good way to sell the stocks is to guarantee a certain per cent., especially for the first year. The stocks are easily sold if they are given to stock brokers, who of course charge extra for this work. Another good idea is to give the broker an interest in the company. Firms who sell stocks you will find in the second part, under Stock Brokers; and addresses of Stock Certificate Printers under Bonds and Certificates.

It is not advisable to found the company on too small a scale, in proportion to the patent. The inventor generally receives a royalty, his selling price in stocks mostly, and has an important position, like superintendent, director, etc.

How easy it often is to found a stock company for the manufacture of a patent, the following proves:

Several years ago a poor German chemist came to the United States. He had invented a new chemical process to make a certain chemical product out of other elements, and much cheaper than it had ever been done before. He found somebody who lent him, on his apparatus and books, for very high per cents (I believe 40), a certain sum of money. With this he had his invention patented. Then he went to a patent agent who said he would sell his patent. The poor inventor had to pay some twenty dollars in advance, but all without luck. He was in a very helpless state, without money, his books and invention mortgaged, knowing very little of the language and habits of America. At last he went to another man. This man, though a German also, had been in this country for some time and knew its language and ways. He promised to help. The inventor, after a few days, went again to the man's house where he found some other gentlemen, one a pretty good chemist. The inventor showed him the process and all was found to be right. They formed an association and sold their stocks easily, because they offered an interest of 14 per cent. the first year. At the beginning they had only enough to pay the corporation and printing expenses. But then they built and manufactured, and in a few years they all were rich.

I think such corporations are founded nearly every day and generally have success. The ground work and success depend entirely upon the value of the patent.

CHAPTER XVII.

WHAT IS THE BEST WAY TO INTRODUCE PATENTS?

In answer to this question we must leave the firm ground of objective and step on the unsafe of subjective views. Out of this we can see that we can say nothing positive, and can only suggest a pattern for a frame which may be arranged to fit each picture. To divide the most plentiful material, even the least bit, we must separate it into two classes, in business patents and speculation patents. Under the first head we will understand such patents whose inventor is in some business, and can and will use it in his own store; or those that went into the hands of a business man for this reason or purpose With the name of speculation patents we endow a great class of patents which are in the hands of neutral persons for selling, and those which are not yet in the hands of one who will make use of them.

We will turn at first to the business patents and remark right away that these must of course be good, useful patents.

The following rules, in which we will try to tell the business patent holder what he shall and what he shall not do, are only in regard to those which are useful.

1. "Try the invention thoroughly before thinking of bringing it to market for sale."

Too often it happens that a patent holder cannot wait, being in such a hurry that he publishes descriptions and uses of it while he is yet experimenting with it. If people wish to buy the article then, he must either tell them that it is not yet complete or he will sell it to them so and cheat them. Then it does not take long before all newspapers and other inventors commence abusing the patent. When the inventor then finishes the improvements on his article, and puts it before the public, it takes long before he can get anybody to believe him.

2. "Try to make the article as good and cheap as possible."

To be able to do both these things at once it is ncessary in most cases to make as many of the articles as possible, and then find a place to dispose of them, and

3. "Seek to interest many people, in fact as many as possible, in it."

By giving high profits to agents, and putting your own profit as low as possible, is the soonest way to attain this result. It is better to make much, good and cheap, with little profit on each, than little, good and expensive, with high profit on each piece. For when much is manufactured at once it can be done more evenly and better, because the work can be divided.

4. "Use the press to advertise."

Through discussions in good papers you can interest many for the article, and through solid advertisements can support the sellers.

5. "If the worth and subject of the article allows you to have, (besides the agents and again sellers,) traveling agents, it is recommended to do so at the beginning. In all cases the inventor must send it to the exposition, as this helps more than is generally supposed. Going to speculation patents, we will mention the following as the best and most useful ways."

1. "Make the patented article first and not spend time and money to get people to interest themselves in an article which is only described on paper."

This is not only to be observed by transportable things but also by original treatments. As soon as you are able to show one perfect apparatus or certificates of the good this or that improvement did, you can sell or find good agents much sooner. If you can pay some money you should always lead your own invention, for nobody can make an article sell so good as the inventor himself.

2. "Bring the patent to market first in you own country, and then, supported by the good luck here, proceed with the foreign patents, if you have any."

On this little patience trial many inventions have already been wrecked. Most inventors, immediately after getting into possession of their patent, believe that everybody knows the patent as well as they. With great expectations they proclaim it in all countries, and as no recommendations are there, nobody will buy it. Little by little the inventor looses courage, and with it all his friends and helpers, who are discouraged, for all their assistance did no good. At last the whole thing is gone and the inventor has only his paper patent, perhaps debts, and anger in his heart for his mistaken genius.

3. " Do not ask too high prices."

The wish of most inventors is to sell their patents fast and high priced. We cannot be angry at them for this. It is unnatural for the purchaser of a patent to buy it for all time, for who can guarantee that the inventor will not make a new improvement on it and then sell that to another. Besides this, nobody knows if an invention that is good to-day may be useless to-morrow, for a new invention may appear which is much better than the old one. The money paid would then be thrown away. I can advise the following and believe it would be perfectly just for both parties : "A small sum to be paid to the inventor for his trouble and expenses, and then a certain part of every article he sells. In short, all that was said in regard to business patents can be used here too, especially the use of the press and the sending to the exposition, to wake the interest and call the attention of the public to the new patent.

CHAPTER XVIII.

ABOUT ADVERTISEMENTS.

A FITTING advertisement is good for the best inventions, perhaps even necessary. Advertisements are a great ruling power now-a-days; the most extensive and most effective branch of papers for this purpose being the political dailies and weeklies. Insertions in the editorial columns are always better than among the advertisements. For really good inventions the newspapers print for nothing if you give them the fitting text and cuts. If the public in general should be interested, daily and weekly papers and periodicals are best. But if experts are to be attracted scientific and technical papers are to be preferred.

Besides newspapers there are many other ways of advertising, and I am sure every inventor will find the right way. One of the best advertisements of small articles was that of the blacking maker, Warren, in London. He had an advertisement written on the Egyptian pyramids, "Buy Warren's shoe blacking. It is the best in the world." Every body scolded on account of the profanation, but he was known now, and in a little while became a rich man.

A very good way of advertising is that of giving lectures to a chosen public, about the uses and advantages of the article.

Another good way is to send an article or a model of it to an exhibition. A bad side of this is, the great expense which sometimes can not even be paid by all the good the exhibition of the article does. If one sends an article to such an international exhibition the article must have international value if one would gain anything by sending it there ; also, the factory must be so located that the goods can be sent to all sections without trouble.

A small compensation for the trouble of sending to the exhibition is their premiums. Though they do not always have a good moral influence on the receiver, still they are good advertisements and are better than most others. Advertisements are to-day worth more than cash and generally must be bought with it. Large firms hate to be without their paper, on whose pages all their patents and premiums are mentioned, and they are right.

When we now look at the list of more or less solid and respectable helps which are in reach of the inventor and manufacturer, we see a whole system. Between the simple newspaper notice and the openly bestowed premium are hundreds of other ways to attract the attention of the public.

He who understands the whole art of advertising will always win, even if the article he sells is no better or of a worse kind than that of his competitor.

CHAPTER XIX.

A GRAND SUCCESS.

About twenty years ago there lived in Provence (France) a workman who liked to read very much. He possessed a library consisting mostly of old novels, which his master had given him. Because he loved them very much and hated to see them so dilapidated, he always thought of a binding and finally devised a self-binder. As it was very useful the pastor advised him to have it patented, which he did, as he had some money. But when he got the patent he did not have any money left to manufacture it. He went to his master who said, however, that the patent was a swindle. This was not very encouraging, but he went again to the pastor who told to put the following in the papers:

"1000 frs. are wanted for three years. High per cent. and great security given."

Sure enough many people came, when he borrowed and commenced to manufacture. He employed a book-binder and with his help made a thousand of the self-binders. Then, as nobody bought them, he was obliged to send his help away. He took the self-binders and went peddling trying to sell them, without luck. Then he thought of the advice of an old Jew whom he had met, to give his articles to a wholesale house for Article de Paris. He went there and offered them the thousand self-binders, but they would only keep them on sale and not buy them. He went from house to house with no better luck. At last he left them at one house and went home to work as before. He had made a contract with the firm that the net profit should be divided.

Not long did he stay on his farm Already, after fourteen days, he received a letter containing 2000 francs and ordering many self-binders, also saying that they would pay cash. One order was quickly followed by another. He founded a book-binder shop, and later on a book bindery works with machine power. And out of this simple beginning, in a short time, arose one of the largest book-binding establishments in the world.

CHAPTER XX.

GOOD ADVICE.

The attentive reader of the foregoing will know the summary himself. We believe, however, that the advice which we intend to give here can not be given often enough to show the inventor, and especially him who has nothing to lose, on what a slippery pathway he is walking, as soon as he over-estimates himself and his invention, and does not know when to stop in his hunt for patents.

Inventions and patents are something like a game of hazard, only the public does not see so much of it. As by hazard playing not every body can prosper and keep on prospering, and if one does it is heralded into the world, we must not think of the many who go to their destruction at gambling tables; so it is with inventions. The few who have won respect and fortunes through them are countable, but those who through their patent and invention craze have nearly, if not entirely, destroyed themselves and their families, are countless.

I do not wish to warn people not to invent. I only want them not to patent carelessly, and ask to warn them against speculation-invention Every one who seeks to improve and help science in any way does nothing wrong as long as he does not get out of reasonable bounds. However, he who believes that he is a grand inventor and when he invents even the most invaluable thing and advertises it in every country, he is a systematic hazard player and ought to be stopped. I warn the small man, not to think his invention is the grandest on earth and worthy to be patented in every country. I also warn the rich inventor, who spends the national wealth in foreign lands because he patents his invention in every nation.

Money for which goods are bought in foreign lands is not wasted; it does some if very little good; but money which is spent on patents in foreign countries has no value to the nation at all. And how easy a patent gets void. As I once before mentioned, every foreign patent is declared void as soon as one of them is allowed to expire. In the same place it is mentioned that in some countries the patent must be manufactured after the expiration of a given length of time. Also, that sometimes a tax must be paid after the patent is granted or it is void. On account of these reasons not more than ten per cent. of all patents gain the age of five years, and not one per cent. live to mature age. Every inventor should well consider before he undertakes to apply for foreign patents, for they are too easily lost. Patents are not so easily taken care of as patentees and inventors at first suppose they are.

Where do those three rules work?

In all countries except Germany the first one is enforced The second is in nearly every country; also the third.

The inventor who, besides his American patent, has one in England, Belgium, Italy, Austria, France and Germany, if he now would let the English patent expire all the others except in Germany would be declared void.

Therefore try your patent first and find out whether it is really worth patenting in any other land. Then take only a few and in countries where they will be valuable. Find out what competent people think of it before you patent it.

Mostly there is no reason to apply too soon. Wait till you have one in your own country, and then if that sells good, try another. Only in very few cases and only with great inventions it is necessary to seek for all patents in quick succession. In other cases keep cool and never over-estimate.

CHAPTER XXI.

MODEL CONTRCTS.

No. 1.

CONTRACT

between Mr. X (buyer) and Mr. Y (seller) in regard to the selling of Patent No. .... of .... on ....

§ 1.

Mr. Y. resigns with this his interest in sub No...... of .... , given patent to Mr. X under the below mentioned conditions, and allows the circumscription of the patent on the patent roll to Mr. X.

§ 2.

Mr. X pays Mr. Y, as payment for that under sub § 1 described patent:

1st. A sum of $ .... , payable in .... installments etc., the first installment payable immediately, the second on .... etc.

2nd. During the continuance of this agreement, only till the end of the patent however, a commission of .... per cent of net selling price of every sold patent apparatus (or of those amounts paid to Mr. X by a third party for the use of a patent treatment.)

The account will be settled every quarter (or half year) The money then due to Mr. Y is to be paid at the latest, on .. .. in cash.

For the control of the commission Mr. X will keep an account book, in which these things shall be entered. This book shall be at the disposal of Mr. Y, or his agent, every month, (or quarter.) Also, every patent article shall be marked with a continued number.

§ 3.

Mr. X is obliged, during the continuance of this contract, to do everything in his power to keep the patent going. Especially he shall be held to the payment of all the patent taxes punctually. If Mr. X should be careless and forget anything, through which carelessness the patent gets void, he shall pay Mr. Y a sum of $ ....

Mr. Y binds himself to help Mr. X, without charge, with his advice, as far as the arrangement of the factory and the use of the patented article or the sustenance of the patent is concerned. Mr. Y furthermore binds himself to give any possible improvement, that he may make to Mr. X free of charge, and the latter is obliged to see that those said improvements are protected by a patent.

(Here can be added a subject on the making of construction drawings, if the inventor can make them.)

§ 4.

The sum named in § 2 of .... per cent shall, from the beginning of the third (fourth) year, be $ .... (not too high a sum), and shall then rise to $ ....

At the end of the year that the royalty does not reach this sum, Mr, X (buyer) may either give the contract, with all rights mentioned in § 3, back to Mr. Y (seller), without an indemnification, or he can raise the royalty to the said sum himself. Patent articles which Mr. X may have on hand or which are yet in manufacture, after the return of the patent to Mr. Y, may be finished and sold within the first three years, with the increase of 25 per cent. on the royalty, stated in § 2, on each article, (raised because patent tax is no more paid).

If the patent falls back to Mr. Y, he can do with it what he wants, and Mr. X is obliged to allow circumscription in case it is again sold.

§ 5.

In case of quarrels both parties are free to bring the case before a court of arbitration, in which case both sides must choose each two arbitrators and these one foreman. Their decision must be taken, however; or the case can be laid before the court nearest to Mr. X's residence.

§ 6.

This contract will be made in ...... copies, and the contracting parties divide the cost equally between them.

Witnesses :

....

....

No II.

These articles of agreement made and entered into this .... day of .... A. D., 18..., by and between Mr. X (seller) and Mr. Y (purchaser), both of the city of .... , Witness: Whereas, Mr. X is now the sole owner and proprietor of a patent and invention of a certain .... , known and patented under the name of .... and, Whereas Mr. Y is desirous to obtain exclusive right and privilege from the said **Mr.** X to manufacture and sell said ...., known as the "........ ......" Now therefore this agreement Witnesses:

That Mr. X, for and in consideration of the premises hereinafter mentioned, does hereby agree to sell and set over unto Mr. Y the exclusive right and privilege to manufacture said .... and the exclusive right and privilege to sell the same in the United States, and all foreign countries, dominions and states for the period of .... years from the date hereof, reserving to himself during that period the ownership of said patent only.

The said Mr. Y, for and in consideration of the premises herein contained agrees to manufacture and sell said ... . , known as the " ...." during said period, and to use the utmost endeavor and vigilance in the manufacture and sale of the same, that his means will permit.

The said Mr. X, as and for his portion of the

capital stock, shall furnish the invention and any possible later invented improvements of said .. .. , known as " ...."; and the said Mr. Y shall furnish all the material, labor and capital required for the manufacture and sale of said .... during the period above mentioned.

And it is further agreed and understood by and between the parties hereto, that all gains, profits and increase that shall come good or arise from or by means of the manufacture and sale of said............ shall be divided between them in even and equal portions, each to receive one half of said profit and gains, and that all losses that shall happen in and by said manufacture and sale thereof, by ill commodities, bad debts or otherwise, shall be borne and paid by the said Mr. Y alone.

And it is agreed by and between the said parties, that there shall be had and kept at all times during the period above mentioned, just, perfect and true books of account, wherein shall be entered and set down all money by him received, paid or expended in and about the manufacture and sale of said ...., as all goods, commodities and merchandise, by him or either of them bought, and all other matters and things whatsoever to the said business and management thereof in any wise belonging, which said books shall be used in common between said parties so that either of them may have access thereto without any hindrance or interruption of the other , and also, that the said Mr. Y, on the first day of each and every month during the continuance of the period aforesaid, shall yield, make and render to the said Mr. X, a true, just and perfect inventory and account of all profits and increase by him made, and all things by him received, disbursed, done or suffered, and all losses by him sustained in the manufacture and sale as aforesaid, and at the time of rendering such account to-wit: On the first day of each month shall pay and deliver to the said Mr. X his just share of the profits made and received.

And it is further mutually agreed between the parties hereto, that in case of the death of the said Mr. X., the said Mr. Y. shall pay to the widow, heirs or representatives of the said Mr. X. from the time of the death of Mr. X. until the end of the period of .... years, ... per cent. of the gain and profits arising thenceforth from the sale and manufacture of the said ...., and in case of the death of said Mr. Y. during the period aforesaid, all rights and privileges to the manufacture and sale of said ...., herein vested in the said Mr. Y., shall revert to the said Mr. X.

And at the end of said period of .... years the said Mr. Y. shall make a true, just and final account of all things relating to said manufacture and sale of the ...., and in all things truly adjust and pay over to the said Mr. X. his share of the gains and profits as herein agreed.

And the said Mr. X. agrees that at the expiration of said term, or in case of the death of the said Mr. Y., or in case of the forfeiture by the said Mr. Y. of the rights and privileges herein granted to him by reason of any non-compliance with the agreement herein, he will buy of the said Mr. Y, his heirs, or representatives, all the material and stock remaining on hand belonging to and used in the manufacture of said ...., and will pay therefor the cost price thereof.

It is further agreed that the said Mr. Y shall make due endeavor to purchase all necessary material at the cheapest prices obtainable, and that the said Mr. X have authority to purchase material for said manufacture of said .... if he can obtain the same at lower prices than the said Mr. Y shall procure them, and that the said Mr. Y, before purchasing such material shall first obtain the consent of the said Mr. X.

In witness whereof the said parties hereto have set their hands and seals this .... day of ... . A. D. 18......

Mr. X......... ......
Mr. Y. ....

In presence of

....

....

Part Second.

ADDRESSES.

AGENTS FOR MANUFACTURERS.

Montgomery, Ala: Warren & Holt
Little Rock, Ark: Colburn E. L.
Pine Pluff, Ark: Colburn E. L.
                Parker & Atkinson
Denver, Colo: Johnson D. M. & Co
                Kelly J. O.
                Kimball & Handley
                Morse E. E.
                Robertson A.
                Shandal T. J.
                Thayer T. S.
                Wood J. H.
Athens, Ga: Bloomfield R. L.
Chicago, Ill: Abbott, J. H. 25 Washington st
              Brown W. C., 45 Lasalle
              Buss & Norton, 414 Phœnix building
              Caldwell Commission Co
              Childs H. K. & Co, 221 5th av
              Freeman A., 139 Lake
              Gates H. F. & Co, 221 5th av
              Gurney C. H. & Co, 247 Lake
              Gustroff A., 92 Lasalle
              Hawes A., 411 Phœnix building
              Hinkley S. P., 45 Lasalle
              Lewis G. F., 67 Washington
              Mihills M. A., 89 Lake
              Miles M. & Son, 138 Jackson
              Munger H. H., 142 Lake
              Reed G. W. & Co, 66 Wabash av
              Rich F. A., 23 S. Canal
              Smith F. W., 137 Lake
              Smith S. A., 23 S. Canal
              Stoner I., 19 Wabash av
              Straus M. & Bro, 19 Wabash av

Taylor J. & Co, 221 5th av
Washington L., 228 5th av
Wells B. W., 107 Dearborn
Williams G. F., 436 Rookery building
Wynne J., 239 Jackson
Ziesler I., 221 5th av
Des Moines, Iowa: Johnson D. M.
Louisville, Ky: Burrell F. R.
Coleman T. C.
Dick A. M.
Frankel H. U.
Gardner C. H.
Gividen B. T.
Gooch T. C. jr
Heelskamp J. G.
Huber & Allison
Moore S. T. & Co
Osborn, Symmes & Co
Pope S. S.
Powell J. D.
Rogers G. M.
Stucky H. F.
New Orleans, La: Anderson J. W., 129 Poydras
Blanchard J. G., 17 Tchoupitoulas
Bobb J. M., 55 Gravier
Bowling N. & Co, 40 Magazine
Burruss W. M., 80 Magazine
Curtis D. M., 17 Tchoupitoulas
Dennery T., 80 Customhouse
Devan, Urquhart & Co, 72 Camp
Evans Bros, 13 Perdido
Gould & Hotter, Bank place
Hampton J. T., 37 Natchez
Hoffman & Fatjo, 71 Tchoupitoulas
Howard G. W. & Co, 796 Magazine
McClure & Ridpath, 73 Poydras
Morphy A. E., 91 Magazine
Parker A. A., 23 Camp
Pring B. H., 188 Gravier
Seymour W. D., 53 Gravier
Thayer C. H. & Co, 54 Magazine
Tupper Bros, 8 Union
Walker F. & Co, 117 Tchoupitoulas
Wolfe U., 65 Magazine
Zeigler J. J., 57 Magazine
Baltimore, Md: Adler H. M., 304 W Baltimore
Blondheim S. S., 29 W Baltimore
Doyle C. J., 14 W German

Baltimore, Md: Loane E. D., 12 N. Charles
Marston L. W. & Co, Light c. German
Patterson G. F. & Co, 217 E Fayette
Ports J. W., 29 W Lombard
Ward S. M., 12 N Charles
Wolf M. W. & Co, 294 W German
Wysham G. F., 16 W Lombard
Detroit, Mich : Anspach & Simon, 147 Jefferson
Atkinson & Pennewell, 131 Woodward
Atlerbury & Van Court, 82 Grisw'd
Berkery J. S., 21 Buhl blk
Bigelow & Gibbings, 153 Jefferson
Cohen D., 32 Walker blk
Cohen M., 32 Walker blk
Dickey J. A., 25 Congress W.
Emery R., 58 Griswold
Huyette & McKay, 333 Lafayette av
Kaeding W. C., 31 Monroe
Middlebrook H. & Co, 91 Jefferson
Ridgely R. B., 42 Woodbridge
Swift Mfr.'s Agency, 47 Rowland
Kansas City, Mo: Supply Am. Co, 416 Am. Bank bldg
Clark W. E. & Bro. 610 Walnut
DaCosta A. M., 126 N 6th
Davenport L. M. & Co 107 Ex bldg
Ganse T. D. 1416 W 11th
Keefer H. A., 26 Gibraltar bldg
Levy L. & J., 211 Alamo bldg
Meacham H. S.1228 W 11th
Rice M., 605 Delaware
St. Louis, Mo: Allison J. W., 205 Pine
Alofs W. L., 707 Olive
Arnheiter C. J., 707 Olive
Bateson C. E. & Bro 825 Lucas av
Bernstein M., 414 Washington av
Cain P. R., 701 Washington av
Clarkson J. H., 506 Olive
Conroy Bro, 208 S 4th
Conway J. H., 608 N 4th
Dillenberg D., 500 N 2d
Farrar B. G. & Co, 623 N Main
Field W. B., 415 N 7th
Fife C. R. 114 N 4th
Forward C. J., 200 S Commercial
Frazer W. O., 203 N 3d
Gibson G. G., 310 N 7th
Goodwin J. P., 516 N 3d
Hazelton H., 619 N 4th

St. Louis, Mo: . . Holmes C. H. & Co, 520 Olive
Howe J. C., 24 N 3d
Jungk H., 113 Olive
Kory M., 618 Washington av
Ladd J. A., 203 N 2d
Levy D., 604 Washington av
McDonald R. E., 400 N 3d
Milburn W., 214 Pine
Pratt C. N., 624 Locust
Rashcoe H., 219 Olive
Schloss T. D., 220 Pine
Shryock W. P. & Son, 414 Wash'n av
Todd G. W., 608 N 4th
Waterman H. D. & S. J., 612 N 3d
Werner J. M., 509 N 6th
Werner M., 509 N 6th
West R. P., 413 Lucas av
White T. C., 421 Olive
Winslow W. A.. 607 N 3d
Woodsworth & Co, 218 N 4th

Omaha, Neb:........Mills, Rankin & Co, 315 Dodge
Phelps A. A. & Co, 10 Bushman blk
Ulrich & Stewart, 409 Paxton blk
Welshans W. J., 311 S 16th

New York City :.....Allen J. L. M., 22 Gold
Anthony H. M., 100 Reade
Aughiltree J. W., 56 Worth,
Baldwin F., 33 South,
Ball E. M. & Co, 49 Leonard
Barbey G. H., 17 Platt
Barton E. E., 27 South
Bateson, Armstrong & Dowd 116 Franklin
Beale & Co, 75 Worth
Beardsley F. W., 173 Greenwich
Bedell S. C., 108 Worth
Bedford & Kellum, 280 Broadway
Bishop A. J., 26 University Pl
Black Foster Co, (Ltd) 279 Church
Bradenburg C. W., 125 Chambers
Breinig G. M., 240 Pearl
Brewster F. C., 56 Worth
Briggs & Co, 318 Broadway
Burnhans R. O., 121 Leonard
Burling W. C., 216 Church
Burnham E. S., 84 W Broadway
Bush M. L., 7 Murray
Capen R. S., 795 Broadway

New York City: ... Carhart F., 113 Worth
Carpenter S. S., 51 Leonard
Chalmers H., 335 Broadway
Champlin C., 22 Platt
Chesebro & Garnsey, 264 Canal
Christensen Rudolph, 90 Chambers
Christie A., 28 White
Clark J. H., 401 Broadway
Clarke A. H., 84 w Broadway
Clark W. C., 280 Broadway
Coffey H. Y., 22 Thomas
Coles J. E. & Co 43 Jay
Conover C. E. Co, 101 Franklin
Cooper G., 98 Fulton
Croghan L. A., 107 Franklin
Culin C. G., 99 Franklin
Cumming & Becker, 275 Church
Damerel G., 18 Cortlandt
Dana R. H. & Co, 25 Beaver
Davie H. B.s, 115 Worth
Davison H. C., 229 Broadway
Day E. T., 192 Broadway
Day J. F., 125 Chambers
Dodman W., 107 Chambers
Domeyer F., 376 Canal
Donnelly D. A., 122 Duane
Dowd P. A. & Co, 239 Broadway
Eckmeyer & Co, 42 Beaver
Farquhar N. & Co, 24 State
Felch F. W., 51 Leonard
Fenton D. W., 163 Maiden lane
Ferguson A. S. & Co, 7 Park place
Ferguson J. B., 115 Worth
Field & Wagener, 115 Worth
Foerster W. & Co, 137 Duane
Foreign Trades Agency (Ltd), 128 Pearl
Francklyn R. & Co, 5 S William
Fraser C. A., 178 Broadway
Friedman J., 48 Murray
Froment Frank L., (Iron), 112 John
Fry G. W. 39 Barclay
Gay John F., 7 & 9 W Broadway
Geriken H. J., 115 Broadway
Gordon F. P., 140 Nassau
Gordon J. E., 39 Barclay
Graff A. M., 99 Franklin
Graffin A. J., 56 Worth
Graffin C. W., 56 Worth

New York City :......Graham J. H. 113 Chambers
Greene J. R., 18 Cortlandt
Griswold M. W., 27 Beekman
Guild A., 56 Worth
Guthrie B. W., 1285 Broadway
Guyon C. F. & Co, 99 Reade
Haager J., 24 State
Haight A. S., 119 Franklin
Hall G. W.. 115 Broadway
Hall J. D., 176 Broadway
Halpin J. J., 83 Chambers
Hammond H. D., 51 Leonard
Harrington A. W., 69 Duane
Harton T. A. E Co, 84 Franklin
Harwood W. B., 23 Murray
Haslam & Hanks, 99 Franklin
Haswell H., 99 Nassau
Hauschild & Esche 335 Broadway
Hawthorn & Co, 12 Courtlandt
Haydock J., 332 Broadway
Heller R. M., 216 Church
Hendrickson I. C., 237 Broadway
Heuacker J. E. 67 Barclay
Herzog T., 79 Leonard
Hicks Bros, 42 White
Hinman Bros, 359 Broadway
Hitchcock J. F., 297 Broadway
Hockmeyer Bros, 116 Franklin
Holden H., 513 Broadway
Holton E. C., 771 Broadway
Hughes G. F., 51 Leonard
Hurst J. N., 115 Worth
Hyde G. H., 712 Broadway
Hyer & Co, 335 Broadway
Hymes D., 118 Chambers
Jacoby C., 554 Broadway
Jenkins J. G., 8 Thomas
Jennings H. D., 34 Thomas
Judd F. F., 235 Greenwich
Kautsky K., 251 Broadway
Keep J. M., 183 Greenwich
Ketcham E., 103 Maiden lane
Klug F., 460 Broome
Kunz H., 122 Duane
Kutnow G., 658 Broadway
Lang O., 115 Worth
Lautenbach S., 323 Church
Lavendol E., 99 Franklin

New York City : . . Lebel & Fisk, 4 College pl.
Levene & Co, 53 Franklin
Libbey B. E, 117 Waverly pl
Lord J. B., 115 Worth
Lyons A., 36 Maiden lane
McClain & Talbot, 110 Worth
McCoy H. E., 56 Worth
McCrea J. E., 316 Church
McCreery W. A, 99 Franklin
McKean J., 86 Leonard
Macpherson I. R., 401 Broadway
Maduro S., 63 Murray
Maginnis W. II., 115 Worth
Mallory H. L., 107 Franklin
Mather J. W., 56 Worth
Meeks W. F. & Co, 9 Murray
Merritt G., 94 Liberty
Milliken T. K., 61 Leonard
Muchsam A., 13 w Broadway
Nock G. F., 176 Fulton
Norris W. K., 280 Broadway
Odell C. H., 15 Broad
Otensen C. G. C., 159 Chambers
Otto R. & Co, 102 Chambers
Phipps N. L., 56 Worth
Pittman W. R., 115 Worth
Price E. W., 17 Platt
Raborg H. M., 88 Leonard
Rintoul J., 173 Greenwich
Robbins R. A., 141 Chambers
Robinson B. F., 51 Leonard
Roch L. G., 867 Broadway
Roeder George, 319 Broadway
Rogers H. D. & Co, 75 Maiden lane
Roraback J. O., 335 Broadway
Ross A., 335 Broadway
Ryan T. J. & E., 343 Broadway
Sanders H., 51 Leonard
Schnarr & Delius, 115 Worth
Scott W., 157 Broadway
Sealey A. A., 20 Nassau
Senior T. H., 57 Beekman
Sherman J., 296 Broadway
Silver J. S., 13 Barclay
Simmons W. A. & Co, 13 Barclay
Skirving W. B., 37 Beaver
Smith A. A., 86 Reade
Smith C. A., 409 Broadway

New York City: . . Smith G. V., 104 Reade
Smith & Scherr, 99 Franklin
Smyth J. D., 335 Broadway
Snyder A. H. & Son, 70 Worth
Thatcher E. C., 150 Nassau
Thayer F. P. & Son, 18 Warren
Thompson R., 105 Chambers
Thorpe J., 5 Beekman
Tinagero J. F. & Co, 12 Old st
Tollett E. A., 176 Broadway
Tommins & Adams, 116 Chambers
Umphred Bros & Ferguson, 2314 2d av
Unger H. J., 115 Worth
Valentine & Flagler, 99 Franklin
Vanderbilt and Reynolds, 7 Lispenard
Vorhauer W., 29 Murray
Wade O., 71 Broadway
Wakefield W. L., 77 Franklin
Wallach W., 231 Broadway
Webster C., 57 Leonard
Weir J. D. & Co, 78 Franklin
White T. C., 103 Chambers
Whitney A. R. & Co, 17 Broadway
Whitley & West, 323 Broadway
Whitney D. J., 47 Warren
Wilde C. E., 253 Church
Wiley M., 49 Lispenard
Willard W. A., 33 Chambers
Wilson & Bradbury, 95 Franklin
Winnant J. J., Jr. 32 Thomas
Wootton C. W., 99 Franklin
Wright S., Jr. 20 Lispenard
Zerfass C. E., 39 E 14th

Cincinnati, O:...... ..Chapin D. B., 4 w 2d
Cooke D. McK & Co, 49 w 2d
DeRuiter W. & Co, 15 w 2d
Durrell Bros, 25 w Pearl
Evans & Robertson, Chamber of Commerce building
Fullerton G. W. & Co, 8th c Sycamore
Goshorn A. O., 7 Hammond building
Hume & Beahr, 228 w 4th
Johnston Bros, 264 w 4th
Liebenstein L. K. & Co, 162 w 3d
Males H. W. & Co, 99 w 4th
Mendenhall D., 187 w 4th
Pollock & Co, 322 Main

Cincinnati, O: . . . Putnam, Hooker & Co, 52 w. 2d
Richardson H. M. & Co, 8 w. Pearl
Walter H. H., 107 w. 2d
Wessel, A. 53 w. 2d
White A. & Co, Pike's building
Cleveland, O: ......Billow E. E. & Co., 158 Public square
Carlise M. W., 130 Water
Kennedy W. D. & Co, 122 Water
G. B. Johnson, 121 Superior
Patterson & Co, 45 Euclid av
George G. Wells, 89 St. Clair
Dayton, O: . . . . . Bates W. L.
Lima, O: . . . . . . Moore Brothers
Philadelphia, Pa: . Aaron S. R., 610 Arch
Adams G., 1020 Chestnut
Berry H. A., 20 n. 7th
Bierce C. E., 1020 Chestnut
Brooks A. G., 619 Walnut
Brown T. H., 700 Arch
Bush C., (Iron), Drexel Bldg
Cake B. F., 69 N Front
Clayton T. H., 831 Arch
Clift & Wilcox, 1020 Chestnut
W. W. Commins, 1017 Chestnut
Crawford, W. K., 905 Market
Crowell C. S., 707 Market
DaCosta H. R., 833 Arch
Davis C. S., 114 S. 6th
DeCasseres Elias G. 222 Market
DeCosta H. R. 833 Arch
Dennis G. W., 15 S. 9th
Douglass C. C., 710 Sansom
Ennis C. H, 1020 Chestnut
Fawcett T., 35 Strawberry
Gay L. S., 64 N 4th
Gratz E., 236 Chestnut
Haverstick A, 700 Arch
Henry G. H, 236 Chestnut
Hinman C. C., 407 Walnut
Hofheimer M, 610 Arch
Hopkins & Small, 206 S. 5th
Jackson, Slaymaker & Co, 727 Market
Jenkins, W R., 1020 Chestnut
Kyle J, 109 Front
Lamotte T. A. 415 Commerce
Levy A., 729 Market
Loomis C. H., 1020 Chestnut
Loomis K. H, 430 Walnut

Philadelphia, Pa; McDonnell, C. A., 905 Market
Markley, T. W., 15 S. 9th
Merrill, V., 149 N. 3rd
Middleton A. H., 24 N. Front
Miller W. H., 503 Arch
Mohr J. N., Bullitt Building
Newsome T., 41 Strawberry
Ottey E. H., 1002 Chestnut
Phillips F. R., 407 Walnut
Pollock A., 732 Arch
Raser, S. S., 512 Commerce
Reuben, S. R., 610 Arch
Sheetz & Stephen, Drexel Building
Silberman M., 831 Arch
Simpson, H., Jr., 833 Arch
Smethurst W. A., 7 Bank
Storer G. W., 149 N. 3d
Smith C. W. R., 55 S. 3d
Stern M., 1345 Arch
Swift J. S., 1020 Chestnut
Taylor W. G., 37 S. Front
Thomas, E. H., Bainbridge st. wharf
Tilton W. H., 1023 Market
Walker & Kepler, 108 S. 4th
Walnut T. H., 502 Market
Weatherly W. L., 214 Church
Wilcox H. A., 1020 Chestnut
Wilson S. W., 119 S. 4th
Yerkes S., 622 Chestnut
Pittsburg, Pa:...Beggs H. C., 801 Liberty av
Black H. M. & Co;, 821 Penn av
Camp H. E., 901 Liberty av
Carter, Macy & Co., Penn bldg
Colville W. W. 811 Hamilton bldg
Dalzell A. F., Penn bldg
Davis H. H., 99 Water
Davis E. & J., 115 Water
Deardorff I. L., 702 Penn bldg
De Noon Bros. & Ewing, 5 7th av
Forner W. F., 5 7th av
Gwen J. M., 59 9th
Kirby J. M., (dry goods, notions), 15 7th av
McLean A. C., 52 9th
Magnus J. W., 2 Jackson bldg
Messing & Co., 20 5th av
Overend J. W. (notions), 543 Wood
Price W. P., 137 1st av
Sellers F. & Co., 615 Penn bldg

Pittsburg, Pa :.....Stuart & Corse (dry goods, etc.), 36 6th
Swearingen C., 58 9th
Thirtle J , (boots & shoes), 533 Smithfield
Chattanooga, Tenn : Martendale & Acosta
Galveston, Tex :...Hennessy P. H. & Co
Hughes W. J. & Co
Milwaukee, Wis : Cohen Alex, 587 Jackson St

ARMS.

Los Angelos, Cal : Tufts-Lyons Arms Co
San Francisco, Cal : Jones, McCracken & Co
Denver, Col : ......Hilter & Reedman
Lower J. P. & Sons
Hartford, Conn : Colt's Pat. Fire Arms Mfg Co
The Billings & Spencer Co
The Gatling Gun Co
Meriden, Conn : Parker Bros
New Haven, Conn : N. D. Folsom & Co
Marlin Fire Arms Co
Strong Fire Arms Co
Winchester Repeating Arms Co
Norwich, Conn : Bacon Arms Co
Hopkins & Allen Mfg Co
Chicago, Ill :......Grimm Rudolf
Graff & Jordan
Chicago Gun & Cuttlery Co
Jenny & Graham Gun Co
New Orleans, La : H. & D. Folsom Arms Co
Boston, Mass :....John P. Lovell Arms Co
Worcester, Mass : Foreand & Wadsworth
Harrington and Richardson Arms Co
St. Louis, Mo :.....E. C. Meacham Arms Co
Omaha, Neb :.......The Collins Gun Co
Manchester, N. H : Killey & Wadleigh
Jersey City, N. J : Star Pistol Co
Buffalo, N. Y : ... Buffalo Arms Co
Cortland N. Y:...F. A. Bickford & Co
Ilion, N. Y :........ E. Remington & Sons
Ithaca, N. Y :......Baker, McIntyre & Van Natta
New York City :...Alford & Berkele Co
Merwin, Hurlburt & Co
C. E. Overbaugh & Co
Pneum. Dynamite Gun Co
Wiebuck & Hilger
Rochester, N. Y : W. D. Chapman, Sons & Co
Syracuse, N. Y : Lefever Arms Co
Syracuse Forging & Gun Co
Cincinnati, O :...Brande Arms Co

Cincinnati, O :.....B. Kittridge Arms Co
          Clark, Widdifield & Co
Cleveland, O : .....The Chamberlin Cartridge Co
Hummel's Wharf, Pa : Baum & Co
Nazareth, Pa : .....H. James & Sons
Philadelphia, Pa. : The Foehl & Weeks Fire Arms Mfg Co
          E. K. Tryon, Jr. & Co
Milwaukee, Wis. : J. Meunier Gun Co

BARBERS' AND DENTISTS' CHAIRS.

Chicago, Ill :...... Hornung Mfg Co
St. Louis, Mo :......Koken Barbers' Supply Co
New York City :...Klingler S , 30 S. 5th av
          Schwaab Adam
Rochester, N. Y :..Archer Mfg Co
Canton, O :.........Canton Dental & Surgical Chair Co
Cincinnati, O :... Berninghaus Eugene

BICYCLES AND TRICYCLES.

Hartford, Conn :...Weed Sewing Machine Co
Chicago, Ill :...... Pierre Geo. N., & Co
          Pope Mfg Co
          Western Wheel Works
Boston, Mass :......Wm. Read & Sons
St. Louis, Mo :... St. Louis Wheel Co
          Knight Cycle Co
Newark, N. J. :... H. B. Smith Machine Co
Philadelphia, Pa: Strong & Green Cycle Co
          Sweeting Cycle Co

BILLIARD TABLE MANUFACTURERS.

SanFrancisco,Cal: Brunswicke Billiard Table Manf. Co
Chicago, Ill :........The Brunswick, Balke Collender Co
Boston, Mass :.....Came J. E. & Co
Detroit, Mich :......The Schulenburg Manfg Co
New York City.....Griffith Wm. H. & Co
Cincinnati, O :.....National Billiard Manfg Co

BITTERS MANUFACTURERS.

SanFrancisco,Cal : Ruther & Bendixon
          Sherwood & Sherwood
St. Louis, Mo :.....Home Manfg Co
Louisville, Ky :...Green N. & Co
New York City.....Balfe & Co

BLACKING MANUFACTURERS.

Boston, Mass :.....Brown B. F. & Co
          Cahill M. S. & Co

New York City.....Bixby S. M. & Co
Philadelphia, Pa ; Porpoisine Mnfg Co

BOAT BUILDERS.

Wilmington, Del : Bannar & Munn
                Drein T. & Son
Chicago, Ill :........Kane, Thomas & Son
Detroit, Mich :......Campan S.
Jersey City, N. J : Hofmeyer C. G.
Brooklyn, N. Y :...Ayers Sam
New York City.....Glore Andrew & Son
                Hayes E. A.
Peekskill, N.Y :...Osborn Wm. R.
Troy, N. Y :........Waters S. & Sons

BOILER MAKERS.

Sacramento, Cal : Sacramento Boiler and Iron Works
SanFrancisco,Cal : Risdon Iron and Locomotive Works
Denver, Col : .....Star Boiler and Sheet Iron Works
Waterbury, Conn: Waterbury Steam Boiler Works
Chicago, Ill :......Hazleton Tripod Boiler Co
Fort Wayne, Ind : Bass Foundry and Machine Works
Baltimore, Md :... Poole Robt. & Son Co
Worcester, Mass : Worcester Boiler Works
Minneapolis, Minn : Minneapolis Boiler Co
St Paul, Minn :...Northwestern Boiler Works
St. Louis, Mo :......Rohan Bros. Iron Works
Albany, N. Y :......Ferguson Boiler Co
Buffalo, N. Y :......Lake Erie Boiler Works
Cincinnati, O :.....The Tudor Boiler Manfg Co
Philadelphia, Pa : Harrison Safety Boiler Works
Pittsburgh, Pa :...Lappan James & Co

BOND AND BLANK CERTIFICATES.

Boston, Mass :..... Heliotype Printing Co
New York City... American Bank Note Co

BRASS WORKS.

San Francisco Cal : Roylaure I.
Denver, Col :........Denver Brass Works
Waterbury, Conn:The Plume & Atwood Mfg Co
Belleville, Ill :..... Jones Jam. Mfg Co
Chicago. Ill :........Chicago Brass Works
                Crane Bros. Mfg Co
Louisville, Ky :... Eagle Brass Works
                Novelty Brass Foundry
Boston, Mass:..... Edson Mfg Co
                Foster Wm. T. & Co

Detroit, Mich :......Detroit Sheet Metal & Brass Works
               Galvin Brass & Iron Works
St. Paul, Minn :...Northwestern Copper & Brass Works
St. Louis, Mo :.....Central Union Brass Co
Brooklyn, N. Y :.. Lewis & Fowler Mfg Co
New York City :... Palmenbergs I R , & Sons
               Power Maurice J
Cincinnati, O :.....Lunkenheimer Brass Mfg Co
Cleveland, O ;..... American Bronze Works
Philadelphia, Pa:..Bureau Bros
               Perkers Chas
Pittsburg, Pa :..... Carbon Bronze Co

CAR BUILDERS.

Oakland, Cal :..... Burnham, Standeford & Co
San Francisco, Cal : Carter Bros
Bridgeport, Conn; Rolling Stock Co
Wilmington, Del: Delaware Car works
Jacksonville, Fla: Jacksonville Car Comp
Chicago, Ill :........Arms' Palace Horse Car Co
               Canda Cattle Car Co
               Terre Haute Car Mfg Co
               The U. St. Rolling Stock Co
Pullman, Ill :...... The Pullman Car Comp
Portland, Me :......Portland Co
Detroit, Mich :.....Michigan Car Co
St. Louis, Mo...... Brownell & Wright Car Co
               St. Louis Car Comp
Brooklyn, N. Y :.. Lewis & Fowler Mfg Co
New York City :.. The Harlan & Hollingsworth Co
               The Iron Car Comp
               Stephenson John, Comp
               Union Palace Car Co
               Wagner Palace Car Co
               Woodruff Sleeping & Parlor Car Co
Troy, N. Y :........Gilbert Car Manfg Co
Philadelphia, Pa: The Allison Manfg Co

CARRIAGE AND WAGON MANUFACTURERS.

Montgomery, Ala: Montgomery Carriage Works
San Francisco, Cal :..Sanborn A. W., & Co
               Whaff & Dudley
Denver, Col :........Butler, Wyman & Atwood
               The Robertson & Doll Carriage Co
               Woeber Bro. Carriage Co
New Haven Conn :..Cruttenden & Co
               Hooker Henry, & Co
               New Haven Carriage Co

Chicago, Ill :...... Edwards H. J., & Sons
                    Staver H. C , Mfg Co
                    Weber Wagon Co
South Bend, Ind : Studebaker Bros Manfg Co
Davenport, Iowa : Lamp P. & Co
Topeka, Kansas : Walter J. W. & Son
Louisville, Ky :...Ruby Carriage Manfg Co
New Orleans, La : Garland & Kaler
Portland, Me :......Martin Piennell & Co
Baltimore, Md :...Kunkel John N. & Co
Boston, Mass :.....Colman Moses & Son
                    French Fred. F. & Co
                    Hall James & Son
                    Nichols, D. P. & Co
                    Sargent Francis & Co
Detroit, Mich :.....Columbus Buggy Co
Minneapolis, Minn : Moline Milburn & Stoddard Co
                    Northwestern Impl. and Wagon Co
                    Smith Wagon and Implement Co
St. Paul, Minn : ..Northwestern Wagon and Carriane Co
                    St. Paul Carriage Co
                    St Paul Park Carriage Co
St. Louis, Mo :..... Haydock Brothers
                    Moon Brothers
                    Schelp Wagon and Carriage Co
Omaha, Neb :......Novelty Carriage Works
Newark, N. J :.....Colyer J., & Co
                    Kelly & Co
                    Qumby J. M , & Co
                    Allen & Smith
Albany, N. Y :.....Standard Wagon Co
Brooklyn, N. Y :..Bungarz Stage and Wagon Works
Buffalo, N. Y :..... Strasser Wagon Works
Newbury, N. Y :.. Bazzoni L. J.
Few York City :.. Babcock H. H., Co
                    Borrho Jacob
                    Bradley & Co
                    Demarest A. T., & Co
                    Lowdon & Rutherford
                    Fifth Wheel Co
Poughkeepsie, N. Y :Reed & Dorland
Rochester, N. Y :..Cunningham James, & Son
Syracuse, N. Y :...Whitney Wagon Works
Troy, N. Y :........ Troy Carriage Works
Durham, N. C : Durham Carriage Works
Cincinnati, O :...... Enterprise Carriage Mfg Co
                    Favorite Carriage Co
                    Lippelmann Carriage Co

Cincinnati, O :.....Miller's Geo. C., & Sons
Overman Carriage Co
Cleveland, O :..... Cleveland & Brooklyn Carriage & Wagon
Works
Allegheny. Pa :.... West E., & Sons
Philadelphia, Pa : Braithwait R. M., & Co
Caffrey Chas. S. Co
Hunt William, & Son
Rogers William D., Sons & Co
Union Hub, Spoke and Wheel Co
Pittsburg, Pa :.....Glesencamp L., & Son
Knoxville, Tenn :..Knoxville Buggy Works
Knoxville Carriage Factory
Nashville, Tenn :..Cherry, Morrow & Co
Dallas Tex :........ East Dallas Mfg Works
Salt Lake City, Utah :..People's Implement Co
Richmond, Va :... McDonough J., & Co
Milwaukee, Wis :..Brown T. H., & Co
Milwaukee Buggy Co
Racine, Wis :.......Fish Brothers
Racine Wagon and Carriage Co

CHEMICAL WORKS.

San Francisco, Cal : California Chemical Works
Pacific   "   "
San Francisco "   "
Western Mineral Co
Denver, Colo :.....Colorado Chemical Works
Bridgeport, Conn : Fairfield Chemical Works
Glenbrook, Conn : The C H. Phillips Co
Hartford, Conn : Beach & Co
Sisson T. & Co
Louisville, Ky :...Struss Chemical Works
Baltimore, Md :... Lazaretto Chemical Works
Miller H. S. & Co
Monumental Chemical Co
Boston, Mass .....Egyptian Chemical Co
Enterprise Chemical Co
Detroit, Mich :...Parke Davis & Co
St. Louis, Mo :...Alff Chas. Chemical Works
Davy Chemical Works
Herf & Fredricks Chemical Works
Jersey City, N. J : Tartar Chemical Works
Newark, N. J :.....Hanson, VanWinkle & Co
King Chemical Works
Technical Chemical Works
Albany, N. Y :....Albany Chemical Works
New York City :..American Chemical Works

Atlantic Chemical Co
Borgenport Chemical Co
Crown Chemical Works
New York Organic Chemical Works
Passaic Chemical Works
Union Chemical Works
The Zucker & Levett Chemical Co
Cincinnati, O :..... Berghausen Chemical Co
Central Chemical and Manfacturing Co
The Merrell Chemical Co
Cleveland, O :..... Rosenwasser Laboratory
Standard Chemical Co
Chester, Pa :...... Geo. S Coyne
Philadelphia, Pa : Pennsylvania Chemical Works
Providence, R. I . Rumford Chemical Works
Richmond, Va :... Richmond Chemical Works

ELECTRICAL INSTRUMENTS.

(See also Machines.)

Los Angelos, Cal : Los Angelos Electrical Works
Sacramento, Cal : Pacific Electrical Works
San Diego, Cal : San Diego Electrical Works
San Francisco, Cal : Cal. Electric Light Co
Cal. Electric Works
Electrical Supply Co
Hatteroth & Russ
Ansonia, Conn : . . The Electric Supply Co
Bridgeport, Conn : . New England Electric Supply Co
Star Electric Co
Hartford, Conn : . Billings & Spencer Co
Standard Electric Co
Waterhouse Electric & Mnfg Co
Manchester, Conn: Mather Electric Co
Middleton, Conn : Schuyler Electric Co
New Haven, Conn : H. B Cox Electric Co
Elm City Electric Co
G. H. Simmons
Torrington, Conn : Union Hardware Co
Waterbury, Conn : Connecticut Electric Co
Electr. Appliance Mfg. Co
Standard Electric Time Co
Woolworth & White Co
Windsor, Conn : . Eddy Electric Mfg. Co
Washington, D. C. J. U. Burket
Washington, D C : J. H. Kuehling
G. C. Maynard
Royce & Marean

Atlanta, Ga : . . . Cole, Gentry & Co
Chicago, Ill : . . . American Electric Meter Co
J. Annussen
P. Atkinson
Automat. Temp. Regulating Co
F. Bain
L. S. Baldwin & Co
Belding Motor & Mfg. Co
Bidwell Electric Rasho & Mfg. Co
Central Electric Co
Chicago Electric Service Co
E. Chiles
H. P. Comstock
Cowl & Van Denburgh
G. Cutter
Daft Electric Co
Darche Electric Co
Electric Mfg. Co
Electric Protection Supply Co
Electric Construction Co
The Electric Supply Co
Electro-Optic Mfg. Co
Faraday Carbon Co
Chicago, Ill : . . . Fowler & Co
Franklin Electric Co
J. W. Glass & Co
E. E. Harbert & Co
G. A. Harmount
E. Hoefer
Ill. Angle Am. Storage Battery Co
Knapp Electrical Works
J. Lang & Co
McIntosh Battery & Optical Co
H. Newgard
Nutting Electric Mfg. Co
J. D. O'Neil
The Owen Electr. Belt & Appliance Co
Pumpelly Stor. Bat. & Electr. Motor Co
Sanden Electric Co
Sprague Electric Equipment Co
Standard Underground Cable Co
Western Electric Co
Rockford, Ill : . . . Rockford Electric Mfg. Co
Fort Wayne, Ind : . Star Iron Tower Co
Richmond, Ind : . Home Electric Appliance Co
Terre Haute, Ind : . Electrical Mfg. Co
Davenport, Iowa : . Hawkeye Electric Mfg. Co

Des Moines, Iowa : Hess Electrical Co
F. H. Waiting & Co
Dubuque, Iowa : . Dubuque Electric Works
Topeka, Kansas : . Kansas Electric Co
Louisville, Ky : . Standard Electric Co
Gaynor Electric Co
American Semaphore Co
Baltimore, Md : . . Automatic Switch Co
J. A. Barret Battery Co
Marr Construction Co
Maryland Electric Motor Co
The Pope Electric Co
Southern Electric Co
Attleboro, Mass : . Smith Electric Co
Boston, Mass : . . American Electric Register Co
American Magnetic Electric Co
Automatic Electric Service Co
Boston Electric Co
Campbell Electrical Supply Co
Connelly Electric Heat Regulator Co
Consolidated Electric Mfg. Co
Crosby Electric House Signal Co
C. & C. Electric Motor Co
Eastern Electric Cable Co
Boston, Mass : . . Electrical Accumulator Co
Electric Development & Mfg. Co
The Electric Gas Lighting Co
The Electric & Machine Co
Enos Electric System Co
Eureka Door & Call Bell Co
Gould–Tisdale Railway Signal Co
Gray's Dynamo–Electric Machine Co
Holtzer–Cabot Electric Co
Mansfield Electric Co
National Electric Service Co
Redding Electrical Co
Simple & Electrical Co
U. S. Electric Light & Battery Co
Ziegler Bros
Cambridgeport,Mass : Shaefer Electric Mfg. Co
Malden, Mass : . . B. S. Hale & Son
Taunton, Mass : . Taunton Electrical Supply Co
Detroit, Mich : . . Commercial Electric Co
Detroit Electrical Works
Detroit Motor Co
Electrical Construction Co
Michigan Electric Service Co

Detroit, Mich : . . Michigan Electric Works
Woodward Electrical Co
East Saginaw, Mich : Electrical Supply Co
Grand Rapids, Mich : Peninsular Electric Co
Kalamazoo, Mich : Electro Medical Battery Co
Minneapolis, Minn : Bell Electric Co
Minneapolis Electric & Construction Co
St. Paul, Minn : . . Acme Electric Co
Northern Electr. Construct. & Sup Co
Thompson–Houston Electric Co
Weston Electric Light Co
Kansas City, Mo : . Gate City Electric Co
Southwestern Electrical Supply Co
St. Joseph, Mo : . . St. Joseph Electrical Supply Co
St. Louis, Mo : . . Electric Supply Co
Fidelity Carbon Mfg. Co
St. Louis Electrical Co
Omaha, Nebr : . . . Midland Electric Co
Nebraska Electric Co
L. W. Wolfe & Co
Manchester, N. H : Electrical Machine Co
Camden, N. J : . . Applegate Electric Floor Mat Mfg. Co
Albany, N. Y : . . Electric Mfg. Co
Hamilton Electric Works
Robinson Electric Works
Auburn, N. Y : . . Auburn Electric Supply Co
Brooklyn, N. Y : . Th C. H. Carter Co
Electron Mfg. Co
N. Y. & Brooklyn Electric Co
Buffalo, N. Y : . . . Buffalo Electric Co
G. N. Brown & Co
T. & E. Dickinson
Valentine & Son
New York City : . American Electric Works
Arnon & Hochhauson Electric Co
Barr Electr. Mfg. Co
Abr. L. Bogart
J. H. Bunnell & Co
Complete Electric Construction Co
Electric Construction & Supply Co
Electric Power Controller Co
Electric Signal Mfg. Co
Empire City Electric Co
E. S. Greeley & Co
Hartford Dynamic Co
Herzog Teleseme Co
Jerome Kidder Mfg. Co

New York City : . New York Electric Supply Co
                  Westinghouse Electric Co
Schenectady, N.Y : Edison Machine Works
Syracuse, N. Y : . . Electrical Mfg. Co
Troy, N. Y : . . . . Electric Mfg. Co
Cincinnati, Ohio : . The Homann Model Works
                    Standard Electrical Works
Cleveland, Ohio : . The Cleveland Electrical Mfg. Co
                    Electric Supply & Mfg Co
                    Fletcher & Fletcher
                    The Globe Carbon Co
                    Miller Electric Co
                    The National Carbon Co
                    The Standard Carbon Co
Philadelphia, Pa : Cleverly Electrical Works
                    Eddy Electric Mfg. Co
                    The Electro Dynamic Co
                    Grover Electric Co
                    National Electric Co
                    Novelty Electric Works
                    Quaker City Electric Co
Pittsburg, Pa : . . Electric Supply & Construction Co
                    Empire Electric Carbon Co
                    Keystone Construction Co
                    Westinghouse Electric Co
Providence, R. I : . American Electrical Works
                    Russell Electrical Mfg. Co
Nashville, Tenn : . Electric Fare Box Co
Milwaukee, Wis : . Duerr & Kohn
                   Johnson Electric Service Co

ELEVATOR MANUFACTURERS.

San Francisco, Cal : Cahill & Hall
                     A. J. McNirall & Co
Bridgeport, Conn : Pacific Iron Works
New Haven, Conn : F. C Carmon Mfg. Co
                   The Frisbee Co
Atlanta, Ga : . . . A. B. See Mfg. Co
Chicago, Ill : . . . Crane Elevator Co
                     Ellithorpe Air Brake Co
                     Hale Elevator Co
                     Tuerk Hydraulic Power Co
Louisville, Ky., . Ainslie, Cochran & Co
                   Geiger & Fiske
                   Grainger & Co
                   Louisville Machine & Elevator Works
                   Union Machine Co
Baltimore, Md : . . Bartlett, Hayward & Co

Baltimore, Md : . . James Bates
                    E. Frank & Son
                    Snowden & Cowman
Boston, Mass : . . Elias Brewer
                    L. S. Graves & Son
                    Hawkins Machine Co
                    Holmes & Blanchard
                    Lowell Machine Shop
                    Moore & Wyman
Holyoke, Mass : . Holyoke Machine Works
Detroit, Mich : . . Mich. Elevator & Engine Co
Kansas City, Mo : . The Cookson Iron Works
                    Kansas City Elevator Mfg. Co
St. Louis, Mo : . . John S. Beggs & Co
                    Miller & Saylor
Newark, N. J : . . Currier & Sons
                    Skinner & Leary
Brooklyn, N. Y : . A. B. See Brooklyn
Buffalo, N. Y : . . Howard Iron Works
New York City : . The Ellithorpe Air Brake Co
                    L. S. Graves & Sons
                    Homan Bros. & Couch
                    McGregor Mfg. Co
                    Otis Brothers & Co
Syracuse, N. Y : . . E. W. Houser
Cincinnati, Ohio : The Jas. L. Haven Co
                    C. G. Scott & Co
                    Warner Elevator Mfg. Co
Cleveland, Ohio : The Cleveland Elevator Co
Toledo, Ohio : . . Smith & Haldeman Elevator Co
Philadelphia, Pa : Harrington, Edwinson & Co
                    McCalvey Elevator Works
                    Morse, Williams & Co
                    Richards Elevator Works
                    Stokes & Parish Elevator Co
Pittsburg, Pa : . . Marshall Bros
                    Iron City Elevator & Mach. Works
Milwaukee, Wis : Kieckhefer Elevator Co

FURNACE FACTORIES.

Birmingham, Ala : Alice Furnace Co
Gadsden, Ala : . Coosa Furnace Co
Denver, Colo : . . Colorado Furnace Works
New Haven, Conn : The Raymond Furnace & Mfg. Co
Chicago, Ill : . . The Boynton Furnace Co
                    Butman Furnace Co
                    Magee Furnace Co
                    Peace Furnace Co

Chicago, Ill : . . . Servoss Furnace Co
Boston, Mass : . . Boston Furnace Co
                   Kohler Furnace & Steam Heat Co
New York City : . Earl B. Chace & Co
                   J. L. Mott Iron Works
                   National Stove Co
                   Richardson & Boynton Co
                   The Richardson & Morgan Co
                   The Simonds Mfg. Co
Rochester, N. Y : Eureka Steam Heating Co
Syracuse, N. Y : . Howard Furnace Co
Cincinnati, Ohio : P. Kiefer, Jr., & Bros
                   J. Rink & Son
                   W. Miller Range & Furnace Co
Cleveland, Ohio : Beecher Furnace Co
                   F. & H. Born
                   W. A. Smith & Co
Columbus, Ohio : Columbus Warm Air Furnace Co
                   Vogdsang Furnace Co
Dayton, Ohio : . . Phoenix Iron Works
Toledo, Ohio : . . Isaar D. Snead & Co
Philadelphia,Pa : The Start Peterson Co
                   James P. Wood & Co
Pittsburg, Pa : . . Swindell & Smythe Co
                   Swindell Wm. & Bros
Milwaukee Wis : . L. J. Mueller Furnace Co
                   Schwab & Sercomb

FURNITURE MANUFACTURERS.

San Francisco Cal :West Coast Furniture Co
                   Wolf Braas & Valentin
Denver Colo : . Cooper Hagus Furniture Co
Bridgeport Conn : Furniture Mnfg Co
                   Lieberum Bro
Hartford Conn : . The Hartford Furniture Co
New Haven Conn:The New Haven Rattan Co
Chicago Ill : . . . American Desk & Seating Co
                   Bruschke Furniture Co
                   Chicago Iron Bedstead Co
                   Chicago Parlor Suit Co
                   Crocker Chair Co
                   Halvorson Furniture Co
                   Hildreth Furniture Co
                   National School Furnishing Co
                   W. D Snyder Furniture Co
Louisville Ky : . Kentucky Furniture Mnfg Co
                   Louisville Mnfg Co
Portland Me : . . N. J. Hilln

Baltimore Md: Camden Furniture Co
              The P. Hiss Mnfg Co
              Maryland Furniture Co
Boston Mass: Bardwell Anderson & Co
              Daniels Badger & Co
              Derby & Kilmer Desk Co
              Dorchester Furniture Co
              Fairfield Furniture Co
              New England Furniture Co
              B. C. Noyes & Co
              Quigley Furniture Co
              George F. Roach & Co
Grand Rapids, Mich: Winchester Furniture Co
              Berkey & Gay Furniture Co
              Grand Rapids Chair Co
              McCord & Bradfield Furniture Co
              Phoenix Furniture Co
St. Louis, Mo: Burrell Comstock & Co
              J. H. Conrades Chair Co
              Missouri Furniture Co
              Jos. Peters Furniture Co
              St. Louis Furn. Workers Association
              Western Furniture Co
Albany N. Y: W. A. Choate & Co
Brooklyn N. Y: Brooklyn Furniture Co
Buffalo, N. Y: Buffalo Parlor Furniture Co
              Morgan Furniture Co
              Tifft Furniture Co
New York City: Berkey & Gay Furniture Co
              B. M. Cowperthwait & Co
              Geo. Flint Co
              The Hale & Kilbun Mfg Co
              Herter Bros
              Hoskins & Sewell
              Knapp Sheppard & Co
              J. & J. Kohn
              J. W. Mason & Co
              New York Brass Furniture Co
              The New York Furniture Co
              Pottier Stymus & Co
              W. Schwarzwalder & Co
              Tiffany J. B. & Co
Syracuse N. Y: Syracuse Cab Co
Cincinnati O: The Ahns Mnfg Co
              The Ballman Hugenberg Co
              Central Furniture Association
              Cincinnati Bedstead Co
              Cincinnati Chair Co

Cincinnati, O: . . Front Street Furniture Co
Liberty Furniture Co
Royal Parlor Furniture Co
Cleveland O: . . Cleveland Furniture Co
National Furniture Co
Toledo O: . . . . The Schauss Mnfg
Philadelphia Pa: The Hale Kilburn Mnfg Co
A. Lincoln & Son
Williamsport Furniture Mnfg Co
Pittsburg Pa: . . Danler Close & Johns
Nashville Tenn: . Edgefield & Nashville Mnfg Co
Milwaukee Wis: Farrington Poplar Furniture Co
Northwest Furniture Co
Otto. J. Schoenleber
A. F. Tanner Furniture Co
W. S. Seaman Co
Cream City Furniture Co

GAS AND OIL FACTORIES.

San Diego Cal: . San Diego Trading Co
San Francisco Cal :Am Pat Gas Range & Liq. Fuel Co
T. Day & Co
Chicago Ill: . . . Adams & Westlake Co
American Meter Co
Chicago Gas Stove Co
The Gas Consumer's Protect. Co
The Goodwin Gas Stove and Meter Co
George Harris
Hess Stove Works
G. F. Higgin Manufacturing Co
Maryland Meter and Manufacturing Co
U. S. Oil and Gas Stove Co
Baltimore, Md:. Collins Stove Co
C. Y. Davidson & Co
P. Kries & Co
W. E. Wood & Co
Boston, Mass:. . . Barstow Stove Co
Burrows Manufacturing Co
Champion Gas Heater Co
Dinsmore Manufacturing Co
Florence Machine Co
Generating Gas Stove Co
Maryland Meter and Manufacturing Co
Monitor Oil Stove Co
H. A Norton
W. F. Shaw
Waldo Brothers
C. W. Wheelock & Co

Florence, Mass:. Florence Machine Co
Gardner, Mass:.. American Oil Stove Co
Springfield, Mass: J. L. Griswold
Worcester, Mass: W. H. Thurston
Minneapolis, Minn: Eureka Kerosene and Gas Heater Co
St. Paul, Minn:.. Minnesota Machine Co
     R. Seeger
St. Louis, Mo:.. G. Beck & Co
     Quick Meal Stove Co
     St Louis Gasoline Stove Mfg Co
     Twin Burner Stove Co
     Whorf Gas Stove Co
Brooklyn, N. Y:. Adams & Westlake Co
New York City:. American Gas Pressure Regal. Co
     American Meter Co
     R. E. Dietz Co
     Goodwin Gas Stove and Meter Co
     Sheldon Manufacturing Co
     Union Gas and Oil Stove Co
Cincinnati, O:... American Meter Co
     F. Dieckman
     Werner, Dodd & Co
     Gas Illuminating Co
Cleveland, O:... Daugler Stove Manufacturing Co
     Ohio Gas Heating and Dryer Co
Cleveland, O:... Van Wie Gas Stove Co
Toledo, O:...... R. G Bacon Co
Philadelphia, Pa: Bell & Jones
     The Goodwin Gas Stove and Meter Co
     W. S. Lieber
     H. A. Willes
Providence, R. I: Gas Retort Stove Co
     A. W. Faichild
     Providence Vapor and Oil Stove Co
Milwaukee, Wis: Brand Co The
     Milwaukee Gas Heating Co

HARDWARE, CUTLERY, SPRINGS, ETC.

Berlin, Conn: ... Peck, Stow & Wilcox Co
Birmingham, Conn: The Birmingham Plow Mfg Co
Bridgeport, Conn: E. S. Hotchkiss
     The Smith & Egge Manufacturing Co
Collinsville, Conn: The Collins Co
Hartford, Conn:. The Charles Parker Co
West Winsted, Conn: T. C. Richard's Hardware Co
Chicago, Ill: ... Buffalo Specialty Manufacturing Co
     Capitol Manufacturing Co
     Reading Hardware Co

Dubuque, Iowa:..Schrieber & Couchar Manufacturing Co
Bridgeport, Conn: Bridgeport Spring Co
                Spring Perch Co
                The Fairist Steel Co
Waterbury, Conn: The Henry Spring Co
Chicago, Ill: ....Chicago Tire and Spring Co
                The Rocker Spring Co
Boston, Mass:...The Boston Car Spring Co
St. Louis, Mo: ..St. Louis Spring Co
Cincinnati, O....The Cincinnati Spring Co
New York City .National Car Spring Co
Pittsburg, Pa....The A. French Spring Co

IRON WORKS AND FOUNDERS.

Anniston, Ala...Murray & Stevenson
               Noble Bros & Co
Barton, Ala.....W. H. Cherry & Co
Birmingham, Ala., Aiken & Leighton
               Beggs & Bro
               Birmingham Iron and Machine works
               De Bardelaben & Underwood
               Iron City Foundry and Machine Works
               Linn Iron Works
               Williamson Iron Co
Calera, Ala.....Calera Iron Works
Gadsden, Ala ...Gadsden Foundry and Machine Works
Helena, Ala.....Central Iron Works
Montgomery, Ala., Montgomery Iron works
Opelika, Ala ....Phoenix Iron Works
Selma, Ala......Union Iron Works Co
Shelby Iron Works. Ala., Shelby Iron Co
Stonewall, Ala..Stonewall Iron Works
Tuscaloosa, Ala.Tuscaloosa Foundry Mf'g Co
Little Rock, Ark. Rose City Iron Works
Texarkana, Ark .J. C. Weed & Co
Greenville, Cal..Anderson & Lawrence
Los Angelos, Cal.Baker Iron Works
               Columbia Iron Works
               Conklin Iron Works
               Union Iron Works
Sacramento, Cal.Sacramento Foundry
San Diego, Cal..Standard Iron Works
San Francisco, Cal., American Machine and Model Works
               Architectural Iron Works
               Bay City Iron Works
               California Machine Works
               W. T. Garrett & Co
               Industrial Iron Works

Sacramento,Cal. Main Street Iron Works
                 Marine Iron Works
                 Marshutz & Cantrell
                 Nolte & Walsh
                 G. H. Mixer
                 Rankin, Brayton & Co
                 Rix & Firth
                 Risdon Iron and Locomotive Works
                 Union Iron Works
Stockton, Cal...Globe Foundry and Machine Works
                 Matteson & Williamson
Denver, Colo ...Colorado Iron Works
                 Western Foundry
Fort Collins, Col.Foundry and Machine Co
Ansonia, Conn..Farrell Foundry and Machine Co
Birmingham, Conn., Birmingham Iron Foundry
Brantford, Conn.Malleable Iron Fittings Co
Bridgeport, Conn.Bridgeport Malleable Iron Co
                 The Eaton. Cole & Burnham Co
                 The New Home Manufacturing Co
Hartford, Conn..The Pratt & Whitney Co
Huntsville, Conn.Lyman-Hunt Iron Co
Meriden, Conn..Bradley & Hubbard Manufacturing Co
                 Breckenridge Manufacturing Co
Meriden, Conn..Parker & Whipple Co
Middletown, Conn., W. Douglas
Mystic River, Conn.. Standard Machine Co
New Britain, Conn., The Vulcan Iron Works
                 Union Manufacturing Co
New Haven, Conn.. The G. F. Warner Manufacturing Co
                 The McLagon Foundry Co
New London, Conn.. Albertson & Douglass Machine Co
                 The Brown Cotton Gin Co
                 The Hopson & Chapin Manufacturing Co
Norwalk, Conn..The Simonds Manufacturing Co
                 Lockwood Manufacturing Co
Norwich,Conn..C. B. Rogers & Son
Putnam, Conn ..Putnam Foundry and Mach. Corporation
Stanford, Conn..Stanford Foundry Co
Stonington, Conn., Atwood Machine Co
Wallingford, Conn . Judd Manufacturing Co
Waterbury, Conn ,WaterburyFarrel Foundry and Mach Co
Winsted, Conn.. Winsted Foundry and Machine Co
Sioux Falls, Dak.Sioux Falls Foundry and Machine Co
Newport, Del ...Marshall Iron Co
Wilmington, Del.Phoenix Iron Foundry
Washington, D. C., Potomac Iron Works
Orlando, Fla ....South Florida Foundry and Machine Co

Athens, Ga .....Athens Foundry and Machine Works
Atlanta, Ga.....Van Winkle Gin and Machine Co
                Winship Machine Co
Augusta, Ga....Pendleton Foundry and Machine Co
Columbus, Ga...Columbus Iron Works
Griffin, Ga......Griffin Foundry and Machine Works
Marietta, Ga. ..Phoenix Foundry and Machine Works
Rome, Ga.......Rome Foundry and Machine Works
Savannah, Ga...Kehoe Iron Works
Belleville, Ill.....City Foundry and Machine Works
Chicago, Ill.....Aetna Iron Works
                Aetna Iron and Steel Co
                Aetna Iron and Steel Works
                Ajax Forge Co
                J. H. Bass
                H. J. Berry & Son
                A. Balter & Son
                Bonton Foundry Co
                Brown Brothers Manufacturing Co
                M. C. Bullock Manufacturing Co
                Calumet Foundry Co
                Ohio Forge and Bolt Co
                Dearborn Foundry Co
                Eagle Foundry Co
                Eclipse Manufacturing Co
                Eddy Foundry Co
                Erie City Iron Works
                Excelsior Iron Works
                John Featherstons' Sons
                Gates' Iron Works
                Griffin Wheel and Foundry Co
                Hercules' Iron Works
                Illinois Iron Works
                Illinois Malleable Iron Co
                Illinois Steel Co
                Industrial Iron Works
                Jefferson Foundry Co
                The King & Andrew Co
                Kurtz Bros & Buhrer
                Marinette Iron Works Co
                Michigan Street Iron Foundry
                The J. L. Mott Iron Works
                A. Plamondon Manufacturing Co
                Soper Foundry Co
                South Halstead Street Iron Works
                The Snead & Co Iron Works
                Union Foundry Works
                Vierling, McDowell & Co

Chicago, Ill. ....C. H. Woodruff & Co
Decatur, Ill .....Union Iron Works
Geneva, Ill......The W. H. Howell Co
Joliet. Ill:.......The Joliet Iron and Brass Works
Lake View, Ill...Illinois Malleable Iron Works
Moline, Ill......Moline Malleable Iron Co
          Union Malleable Iron Works
Rock Falls, Ill...Keystone Manufacturing Co
Rockford, Ill ...Union Foundry and Machine Co
Springfield, Ill...Aetna Foundry and Machine Shop
Anderson, Ind...Anderson Foundry and Machine Works
Auburn, Ind ....Auburn Foundry and Machine Shop
Brazil, Ind......Brazil Foundry and Machine Co
Crown Point,Ind.Aetna Iron and Steel Works
Decatur, Ind....Eagle Manufacturing Co
Elkhardt Ind....Elkhardt Iron Works
Fort Wayne, Ind.Bass Foundry and Machine Works
Greencastle, Ind.Greencastle Foundry and Machine Co
Huntington, Ind.Huntington Foundry and Machine Works
Indianapolis, Ind.Eagle Machine Works
          Enterprise Foundry Co
          Indianapolis Foundry Co
          Indianapolis Mfg and Supply Co
Madison, Ind ...Madison Machine Co
Mentone, Ind ...Mentone Machine and Novelty works
New Albany,Ind.Chas. Hegewald & Co
Newcastle, Ind..Newcastle Iron works
Richmond, Ind..Robinson Machine works
Terre Haut, Ind.Phoenix Foundry and Machine works
Burlington, Ia...Murray Iron works Co
Cedar Rapids,Ia.Cedar Rapids Foundry and Machine Co
Chariton, Ia ....Chariton Iron works
Council Bluffs,Ia Council Bluffs Iron works
          Union Iron works
Davenport, Ia...Davenport Foundry and Machine Co
Des Moines, Ia..Des Moines Steam Boiler and Iron wk's
Dubuque, Ia.....Iowa Iron works Co
          Key City Iron works
          Langworthy-Adams Iron works
          Novelty Iron works
Keokuk, Ia. . .Andrus, Loeffler & Co
          Excelsior Sheet Metal works
Le Mars, Ia.... Le Mars Foundry and Machine Shop
Sioux City, Ia...Sioux City Foundry and Machine works
Storm Lake, Ia .Storm Lake Foundry and Machine wk's
Chetopa, Kan ...Co-operative Novelty Iron works
Concordia, Kan .Concordia Foundry works

Enterprise, Kan .J. B. Ersham Machine Co
Fort Scott, Kan. . Fort Scott Foundry and Machine works
Girard, Kan. . . . . Girard Foundry, Machine and Stove Co
Kansas City, Kan. Armourdale Foundry Co
      Consal Iron works Co
      Industrial Iron works
      Union Iron works
McPherson, Kan. McPherson Foundry and Machine Shops
Mound City, Kan. Mound City Manufacturing Co
Ottawa, Kan. . . . . Novelty Iron works
      Ottawa Foundry Co
Parson, Kan. . . . . Parsons' Foundry and Novelty works
Topeka, Kan. . . . Capital Iron works
Ashland, Ky . . . . Ashland Foundry and Machine Shop
      Norton Iron works
Louisville, Ky . . . Ainslie, Cochran & Co
      B. F. Avery & Sons
      Drummond Manuf'g Co
      Fischer-Leaf Co
      Grainger & Co
      Louisville Machine and Elevator works
      The Snead & Co Iron works
Mt. Sterling, Ky. Mt. Sterling Iron Foundry and Mach. Co
New Orleans, La. Whitney Iron works Co
Bangor, Me. . . . . Bangor Foundry and Machine Co
Belfast, Me. . . . . Belfast Machine works
Bridgeton, Me. . Bridgeton Machine Co
Foxcroft, Me. . . . Foxcroft Iron Foundry and Machine Co
Westbrook, Me. . Westbrook Foundry Co
Baltimore, Md . . Baltimore Smelting works
      Bartlett, Hayward & Co
      James Bates
      Central Iron Foundry
      H. Ellicott. H. William & Sons
      Robt. Poole & Son Co
      Isaac A. Sheppard & Co
      Snowden & Cowman
Adams, Mass. . . . Allen Iron works
Ayer, Mass. . . . . Doherty Machine Co
Boston, Mass. . . . Central Iron Foundry
      Chelmsford Foundry Co
      Fulton Iron Foundry Co
      Highland Foundry Co
      Howard Iron Foundry
      Mechanics' Iron Foundry Co
      G. W. Smith Iron Co
      Taunton Iron works Co
      Tremont Foundry and Machine Co

Boston, Mass.... The Wainwright Mf'g Co of Mass
                    Wolaston Foundry Co
B'dgewater, Mass. Bridgewater Iron Co
Canton, Mass... Kinsley Iron and Machine Co
Carver, Mass.... Ellis Foundry Co
Chelsea, Mass... New York Manufacturing Co
Chicopee, Mass.. Ames Manufacturing Co
Fall River, Mass. Kilburn, Lincoln & Co
Fitchburg, Mass. Simons Rolling Machine Co
Foxboro, Mass... Foxboro Foundry and Machine Co
Greenfield, Mass. Wiley & Russell Manufacturing Co
Haverhill, Mass.. Haverhill Iron Works
Lynn, Mass..... Aetna Iron Foundry
Mansfield, Mass.. Central Iron Foundry
New Bedf'd, Mass. New Bedford Iron Foundry
N'h Adams, Mass. James Hunter & Son
Orange, Mass.... Chase Turbine Manufacturing Co
Salem, Mass.... Salem Foundry and Machine Shop
Springfield, Mass. Hawkins Iron works
Worcester, Mass. Arcade Malleable Iron Co.
                    Worcester Malleable Iron Co

Alpena, Mich.... Alpena Industrial works
Battle Cr'k, Mich. Battle Creek Machine Co
Detroit, Mich . Detroit Bridge and Iron works
                    Dry Dock Engine works
                    Eagle Iron works
                    Enterprise Machine works
                    Frontier Iron and Brass works
                    Fulton Iron and Engine works
                    Murphy Iron works
                    Russell Wheel and Foundry Co
G'd Rapids, Mich. Fox Machine Co
                    Grand Rapids Iron works.
                    F. Hartman & Co
                    Michigan Iron works
                    Valley City Iron works
                    Vulcan Iron works
Hastings, Mich.. Hastings Engine and Iron works
Jackson, Mich.. Jackson Foundry and Machine Co
Kalamazoo, Mich. C. H. Bird & Co
Lansing, Mich... Lansing Iron and Engine works
Ludington, Mich. Industrial Iron works
                    Ludington Iron works
Manistee, Mich . Manistee Iron Works Co
Marquette, Mich. Lakeside Iron works
Menominee, Mich. Menominee Iron works
Montague, Mich. Montague Iron works

Muskegon, Mich . Lake Side Iron Co
Newberry, Mich . Vulcane Furnace Co
Owosso, Mich . . . Owosso Iron works
P't Huron, Mich . Phoenix Iron works
Duluth, Minn . . . Nautcue Iron works
       Phoenix Iron works
Minneapolis, Minn . Crown Iron Works Co
       Herzog Manufacturing Co
       Lockwood, Upton & Co
       Minneapolis Foundry Co
St. Paul, Minn . . Amer'n Manufacturing Co
       Eagle Iron works
       Globe Iron works
       St. Paul Foundry
Winona, Minn . . Novelty Iron works
Jackson, Miss . . . River Foundry and Agricultural works
Carthage, Mo . . . Carthage Foundry and Machine Co
Kansas, Mo . . . . Armourdale Foundry Co
       Central Iron works
       Industrial Iron works
       Kansas City Foundry and Machine Co
       Kaw Valley Iron Works Co
       The Keystone Iron Works Co
       Lloyd Foundry and Machine works
St. Louis, Mo . . . Gust. V. Brecht
       Christopher & Simpson
       Excelsior Foundry and Plating Works
       Missouri Malleable Iron Co
       Novelty Foundry and Mfg Co
       Scherpe & Koen Co
       South St Louis Foundry Co
       Standard Foundry Co
       Union Iron and Foundry Co
Butte City, Mont : Cameron & Aiken
Helena, Mont : . . . . . Helena Iron Works
Omaha, Nebr : . . . . Davis & Cowgill Iron Works
Portsmouth, N. H : Portsmouth Machine Works
Claremont, N. H : . Sullivan Machine Co
Exeter, N. H : . . . . . . Exeter Iron Foundry
       Exeter Machine Works
Keene, N. H : . . . . . . Humphrey Machine Co
Lake Village, N. H : Cole Mfg Co
Nashua, N. H : . . . . . . Nashua Lock Co
Arlington, N. J : . . . . Beckett Foundry and Machine Co
Jersey City, N. J : . . . J. C. Wheel Foundry and Mach. Wks
Mount Holly, N. J : T. C. Alcott & Son
Newark, N. J : . . . . . . Cyrus Currier & Sons
       Essex Iron Works

Newark, N. J :......Franklin Iron Works
Ocean City, N. J:..Lake Mfg Co
Patterson, N. J:.....The Watson Machine Co
                    Union Foundry and Machine Works
Trenton, N. J:......Will H. Baker
                    The Phenix Iron Co
                    Union Iron Works
Albuquerque, N.M: Albuq. Foundry and Machine Co
Albany, N. Y :......J. McKinney & Son
Brooklyn, N. Y: ...Bell and Type Foundry Co
                    Brooklyn City Iron Works
                    The Continental Iron Works
                    Fulton Iron Works
                    Healey Iron Works
                    Hecla Archit. Bronze Iron Works
                    Lewis & Fowler Mfg
                    Progress. Iron Works
                    South Brooklyn Steam Engine Works
                    Taylor Williams & Sons
                    Williamsburg Iron Foundry
Buffalo, N. Y:........Buffalo Cast Iron Pipe Co
                    Eagle Iron Works
                    King Iron Works
                    Geo. W. Tifft Sons & Co
New York City:.....Becket Foundry and Machine Co
                    Samuel S. Bent & Son
                    Birmingham Iron Foundry
                    The E. G. Blakslee Mfg Co
                    Central Forge Works
                    Cheny & Hewlett
                    Clauson & Hoffmeyer
                    Coldwell Iron Works
                    Delameter Iron Works
                    Hecla Archit. Bronze and Iron Works
                    Jackson Archit. Iron Works
                    Jonson Foundry and Machine Co
                    Lincoln Iron Works
                    Manhattan Iron Works Co
                    J. L. Mott Iron Works
                    T. Shriver & Co
                    Union Iron Works
                    Wallis Iron Works
Oswego, N. Y :......Kingsford Foundry and Machine Wks
Poughkeepsie, N. Y: Lane Bros
                    Poughkeepsie Foundry and Machi. Co
Rochester N. Y:.....Co-operative Foundry Co
                    Enterprise Foundry Co
                    Munn Austice & Co

Syracuse, N. Y:......Phœnix Foundry and Machine Co
Porter Mfg Co
Syracuse Malleable Iron Works
Troy, N. Y:.........Fuller & Warren Co
Morrison Colwell & Page
Troy Architect. Iron Works
Troy Malleable Iron Co
Alliance, O: ....Morgan Engineering Co
Bucyrus, O:..........Bucyrus Steam Shovel and Dredge Co
Canton, O:............The Miller Mfg Co
Cincinnati, O:........Blymeyer Iron Works
Excelsior Foundry Co
Globe Foundry Co
The I. & E. Greenwald Co
Hamilton Iron Foundry
The L. James Haven Co
Hoffinghoff & Lane Foundry Co
Lane & Bodley Co
Queen City Foundry
Queen City Machine Works
The Stacey Mfg Co
Sam. C. Tatum & Co
Cleveland, O: ....Bowler & Co
T. H. Brooks & Co
City Foundry Co
Cleveland City Forge and Iron Co
Cleveland Foundry Co
Cleveland Ship Building Co
Excelsior Iron Works Co
The Globe Iron Works Co
The Kilby Mfg Co
Maher & Brayton
Myers Mfg and Foundry Co
Riverside Foundry Works
Standard Foundry and Mfg Co
The Taylor & Boggis Foundry Co
The Variety Iron Works Co
Walker Mfg Co
Thomas D. West Foundry Co
Columbus, O:.........Columbus Machine Co
Eagle Foundry
Simpson Iron Co
South End Foundry
Union Foundry
Dayton, O:............Buckeye Iron and Brass Works
W. P. Callahan & Co
Phœnix Iron Works
Harmer, O:...........Harmer Foundry and Machine Co

Lancaster, O:........Eagle Machine Co
Logan, O:.............Motherwell Iron and Steel Co
Mansfield, O:.........Union Foundry and Machine Works
Marion, O:...........Marion Malleable Iron Works
Middleport, O:......Ohio Machine Co
                Vulcan Machine Co
Portsmouth, O:......Portsmouth Foundry and Machine Wks
Sandusky, O:.........Barney & Kilby
Springfield, O: ......Blakeney Foundry Co
Toledo, O:............Eagle Foundry
                N. Haughton Foundry and Machine Co
                Russell Iron Works
                Toledo Foundry and Machine Co.
                Vulcan Iron Works
Warren, O: ....Ætna Machine Co
Wellston, O: ....Wellston Foundry and Machine Co
Wilmington, O: .....Champion Bridge Co
Portland, Oregon: ..Carroll & Johnson
                Willimette Iron Works
Alleghaney, Pa:.....Thos. Carlin's Sons
                Porter Foundry and Machine Co
                Union Foundry and Machine Co
Altoona, Pa:.........Altoona Iron Co
Emporium, Pa:......Emporium Machine Co
Erie, Pa:..............Erie City Foundry
                Erie Forge Co
                Globe Iron Foundry
                Humboldt Iron Works
                Southside Iron Works
Lindsey, Pa:.........Clayville Mfg Co
Meadville, Pa:......Meadville Vice Co
                Phœnix Iron Works
Oseola, Pa:...........Oseola Mfg Co
Philadelphia, Pa: C. A. Blessing
                E. E. Brown & Co
                L. S. Cassin & Co
                Chambers Bro. & Co
                Chester Foundry and Machine Co
                The J. Samuel Creswell Iron Works
                Flagg, Stanley & Co
                C. Hitzeroth
                James Moore
                North Bro. Mfg Co
                A. Penn Iron Works
                Theo. B Rohrmann
                Schuman & Lynch
                I. A Sheppard & Co
                Southwark Foundry and Machine Co

Philadelphia, Pa:...Tacony Iron and Metal Co
Union Iron Foundry
Thomas Wood & Co
Pittsburg, Pa:...... Fisher Foundry and Machine Co
Jones & Laughlin
Lewis Foundry and Machine Co
The McConway, Torley Co
Machintoch, Hemphill & Co
Marshall Foundry and Construction
National Foundry & Pipe works
Pittsburg Foundry Co
Pittsburg Mfg Co
Reed Foundry Co
Robinson Rea Mfg Co
Sraife Foundry and Machine Co
I. & S. Totten & Hogg
Union Foundry and Machine Co
Reading, Pa:..........F. & M. Mellert Co
Scranton, Pa:........ Green Ridge Iron works
Warren, Pa: ....Struthers, Wells & Co
Wilkesbarre, Pa: ...Dickson Mfg Co
Vulcan Iron Works
Wilkesbarre Iron Works
Hope Valley, R. I: Nichols and Langworthy Machine Co.
Providence, R. I:...Builders Iron Foundry
Corliss Steam Engine Co
Fuller Iron Works
Granger Foundry and Machine Co
New England Butt Co
Phoenix Iron Foundry
Providence Steam Engine Co
R. I. Malleable Iron Works
Chattanooga,Tenn: Cahill Iron Works
Chattanooga Iron Co
Lookout Rolling Mill Co
Providence Steel Works
Roane Iron Co
Vulcan Iron and Nail Works
WarrenCar and Wagon Foundry
Knoxville, Tenn:...Knoxville Iron Co
Knoxville Foundry and Machine Co
Memphis, Tenn:... Gun & Pagin
T. L. Risk & Co
Nashville, Tenn: ...Cherry, Morrow & Co
S. E. Jones & Sons
Novelty Foundry Co
Tenn. Range and Mfg Co
Calvert, Texas:.......Calvert Foundry and Mfg Co

Galveston, Texas: ..C B. Lee & Co
Houston, Texas:.....Wiggins & Simpson
Marshall, Texas: ...Marshall Car and Foundry Co
Tyler, Texas: ....Dilley Foundry and Machine Co
Salt Lake City:......Davis Howe & Co
     Salt Lake Foundry and Machine Co
Rutland, Vt:.........Lincoln Iron Works
     Rutland Foundry & Machine Shop Co
St. Johnsbury, Vt; Acme Iron works
Goshen, Va: ....The Iron and Steel Association
Lynchburg, Va:.....Cleveland & Sons
Norfolk, Va:........Elizabeth Foundry
     Etna Iron works
     Norfolk Iron works
Portsmouth, Va: ...Portsmouth Iron works
Richmond, Va:......Jos. Hall Co
     Old Dominion Iron and Nail works
     Asa Snyder & Co
     Tredegar Iron works
     Vulcan Iron works
Palatine, West Va: Marion Machine works
Eau Claire, Wis:...Phœnix Mfg Co
Milwaukee, Wis:...Edw. P. Allis & Co
     Wm. Bayley & Co
     The Filer Stowell Co.
     Hoffman & Billings Mfg Co
     Moore Mfg and Foundry Co
     The Wilkin Mfg Co

LAMP AND GASBURNER MANUFACTURERS.

Meridien, Conn:... Edward Miller & Co
Newark, N. J. ......The Albo Carbon Light Co
Brooklyn, N. Y: ...James W. Lyon
New York City:....E. P. Gleason Mfg Co
Canton, O:............The Sun Vapor Street Light Co
Philadelphia, Pa:...Chas. Gefrorer
     Henry Schrader
     The Siemens Langren Co
Pittsburg, Pa:........The Albo Carbon Light Co

LAMP AND LANTERN MANUFACTURERS.

San Francisco, Cal: E. Boesch & Co
     A. S. Graf & Co
Meriden, Conn :.....Bradley & Hubbard Mfg Co
     The Chas. Parker Co
     Meriden Britannia Co
     Edw. Miller & Co
Waterbury, Conn: Benedict & Burnham Mfg Co

Waterbury, Conn:..Homes, Booth & Haydens
      Plume & Atwood Mfg Co
Washington, D. C: Breach Loading Lantern Co
Chicago, Ill;........The George Bohner Co
      Cass Lamp works
      Climax Mfg Co
      Chris. Edwards Oil Burner & Mfg Co
      Chicago Gas Lamp Illuminating Co
      Globe Light and Heat Co
      Plume & Atwood Mfg Co
      Railroad Signal Lamp and Lantern Co
      Western Wheeler Reflector Co
Indianopolis, Ind:..Sun Vapor Street Light Co
Boston, Mass:........American Health Supply Co
      Boston Lamp Co
      Craighead and Kintz Mfg Co
      Plume & Atwood Mfg Co
Minneapolis,Minn:Sun Vapor Street Light Co
St. Louis, Mo: ......Franklin Gas Lamp Co
      Kraushaar Lamp and Reflector Co
      F. Meyrose & Co
      S. Louis Lantern Co
New Brunswick, N. J: N. J. Lamp and Bronze works
Brooklyn, N. Y:.....N. Y. Kerosene Gas Light Co
New York City:.....H. S. Almy & Co
      Am. Belgian Lamp Co
      Angle Lamp Co
      Ansonia Brass and Copper Co
      Bartlett Street Lamp Mfg Co
      Bradley & Hubbard Mfg Co
      Clawsen & Hoffmeyer
      E. P. Gleason Mfg Co
      B. Goetz Mfg Co
      Hinrichs & Co
      Holmes, Booth & Haydens
      Kruse & Baron
      Manhatton Brass Co
      The Mitchell & Vance Co
      Rochester Lamp Co
      Ed. Rorke & Co
      L. Straus & Sons
      The U. S. Wenham Pat. Gas Lamp Co
      The U. S. Supply Co
Rochester, N. Y:...Kelly Lamp Co
      Rochester Lantern Co
Syracuse, N. Y:.....Steam Gauge and Lantern Co
Watertown, N. Y:..Hitchcock Lamp Co
Cincinnati, O: ......The Alba Lamp Co

Cincinnati, O : ......The Clipper Mfg Co
                     The Mellenry Co
                     Post & Co
                     Queen City Lamp Co
Cleveland, O:.......Lamp and Brass works
                     W. J. Gordon
                     The Standard Lighting Co
                     Star Oil Burner Co
Columbus, O: ....Columbus Lantern works
Alleghaney, Pa: ...Pittsburg Brass Co
Philadelphia, Pa:...American Reflector Co
                     Mascot Mfg Co
                     C. H. Pascoe & Co
                     The Siemens Lungren Co
                     Standard Gas Lamp Co
                     The Pennsylvania Globe Gas Light Co
                     Wheeler Reflector and Light Co
                     The Neumaun Co
                     Wilhelm & Co
Pittsburg, Pa:........S. Morrow & Co
Milwaukee, Wis:...Loeffelholz & Co

LOCK MANUFACTURERS.

San Francisco, Cal: California Safe and Lock Co
                     Wichell & Richards
                     S. B. Paige & Co
Branford, Conn:...Branford Lock works
Bridgeport, Conn:..The Conwall & Patterson Mfg Co
                     The Smith & Egge Mfg Co
Meriden, Conn :.....The Chas. Parker Co
Middletown, Conn: William Wilcox Mfg Co
New Britain, Conn: Corbin Cabinet Lock Co
New Haven, Conn: Mallory Wheeler Co
Norwalk, Conn :.....Duplex Supply Co
                     Norwalk Lock Co
Terryville, Conn:...Eagle Lock Co
Chicago, Ill :.........Automatic Lock Hook Mfg Co
                     Sargent, Greenleaf & Brooks
                     Yale & Towine Mfg Co
Boston, Mass:........L. L. Bate & Co
                     Commercial Lock Co
                     Wm. Hall & Co
                     Hanson Elevator Lock Co
Newark, N. J: ......Phœnix Lock works
                     The National Lock Washer Co
New York City:.....Champion Safety Lock Co
New York City : .....Eagle Lock Co
                     The Mallory Wheeler Co

New York City : ..... Norwich Lock Mfg Co
                     W. Wilcox Mfg Co
Burton, O : .... Edison Lock Co
Cincinnati, O : .... Cincinnati Safe and Lock Co
                     Consol. Time Lock Co
                     European Lock and Time Co
Cleveland, O : .... Industrial Lock and Mfg Co
                     National Safe and Lock Co
                     Perkins Lock Mfg Co
Geneva O : .... Eagle Lock Co
Philadelphia, Pa : ... Autom. Tumbler Lock Co
                     Miller Lock Co
                     Penn Lock Co
Pittsburg, Pa : .... Brittan, Graham & Mathes
York, Pa : .... York Safe and Lock Co
Providence, R. 1 ; ... New England Butt Co

LOCOMOTIVE BUILDERS.

Birmingham, Ala ; ... Douglas Engine Co
San Francisco, Cal : Risdon Iron and Locomotive Works
                     Union Iron Works
Portland, Me ; .... Portland Co
Mt. Savage, Md ; ..... Mt. Savage Locomotive Works
Boston, Mass : .... Hinkley Locomotive Co
                     Manchester Locomotive Works
Taunton, Mass : ..... Locomotive Manfg Co
South Newmarket, N. H : G. E. Fifield
Paterson, N. J : ...... Cooke Locomotive and Machine Co
                     Grant Locomotive Works
Dunkirk, N. Y : ...... Brooks Locomotive Works
New York City : ..... N. Y. Locomotive Works
                     Strong Locomotive Works
Schenectady, N Y : McQueen Locomotive Works
                     Schenectady Locomotive Works
Alleghany, Pa : ...... Pittsburg Locomotive and Car Works
Philadelphia, Pa : ... The Baldwin Locomotive Works
Pittsburg, Pa : .... H. K. Porter & Co
Providence, R. I : ... R. I. Locomotive Works
Nashville, Tenn : ... Adams & Price
Richmond, Va : ..... Richmond Locomotive and Machine Works

MACHINERY MANUFACTURERS.

(See also Iron Works and Foundries.)

AGRICULTURAL.

Athens, Ala : .... Alabama Agricultural Mnfg Co
Birmingham, Ala : Birmingham Tool and Implement Works
Little Rock, Ark : ... The Dudley E. Jones Co
Texarkana, Ark : ..... Wilkerson C

Sacramento, Cal : ...Bull & Grant Farm Implement Co
San Francisco, Cal:.Oliver Chilled Plow Works
                    Pacific Saw Manufacturing Co
                    Price Jacob
                    South Bend Iron Works
                    Truman, Hooker & Co
                    Wickson G. G., & Co
Stockton, Cal :........Stockton Harvester and Agricult. Works
Denver, Col :......... Kinsey J., Implement Co
Hartford Conn :...... The Collins Company
New Haven, Conn :..Bradley Robt. B., & Co
Fargo, Dak :...........Howland & Sons
Odessa, Del :............Aspril L. V., & Son
Washington, D. C :..Heiskell P. H., Jr., & Co
Jacksonville, Fla :...Hubbard S. B., & Co
Atlanta, Ga :......... Southern Agrl. Works
Alton, Ill :............ Alton Agricult. Works
Chicago, Ill :......... Appleton Mfg Co
                    Austin F. C., Mfg Co
                    Goulds & Caldwell
                    McCormick Harvesting Machine Co
                    Morgan D. S., & Co
                    Rice & Whitacre Mfg Co
                    Silver & Deming Mfg Co
                    The Plano Mfg Co
                    Walter A., Machine Co
                    Warder, Bushnell & Glesner
Quincy, Ill :...........Quincy Agricultural Works
Fort Wayne, Ind :...Horton Mfg Co
Indianapolis, Ind :...The Beedle & Kelly Co
Council Bluffs, Ia :..Marseiles Mfg Co
Davenport, Ia :........Davis I. S., & Sons
Kansas City, Mo :...Trumbull, Reynolds & Allen Mfg Co
Louisville, Ky :......Avery B. F., & Sons
                    Southwestern Agricultural Works
Portland, Me :........ Kelley D. T.
Baltimore, Md :......Dinsmore & Kastendike
                    Whitman E., Sons & Co
Boston, Mass :........ Ames Plow Co
                    Whitman & Barnes Mfg Co
Detroit, Mich :........Rawson Mfg Co
Grand Rapids, Mich: Wheeler & Green
Jackson, Mich :......Michigan Implement and Machine Co
Minneapolis, Minn : Advance Thresher Co
                    The Manufacturers Syndicate
                    The Minneapolis Threshing Machine Co
                    Northwestern Implement and Wagon Co
St. Paul, Minn :..... Mast, Buford & Burwell Co

Kansas City, Mo :... Esterly Harvesting Machine Co
St. Louis, Mo :........ Birdsell Mfg Co
Kingsland & Douglas Mfg Co
Whitman Agricultural Co
Camden, N. J :........Taylor Brothers
Albany, N. Y :........Wheeler & Melick Mnf Co
New York City :.......Alexander L., & Co
The Hagganum Mfg Corporation
Rochester. N. Y :.....Vick James
Troy, N. Y :...........Crandall & Morrison
Canton O :...........Aultman C., A Co
Cleveland, O:.........Luetkemeyer H. W. & Sons
Philadelphia, Pa :...Gardiner John, & Co

CABLE RAILWAY MACHINERY.

Kansas City, Mo :...Industrial Iron Works
Cleveland, O:.........Kilby Mfg Co

ELECTRIC LIGHT.

Manchester, Conn :..Mather Electric Co
Middletown, Conn :..Schuyler Electric Co
Plantsville, Conn :.. Connecticut Motor Co
Windsor, Conn :......Eddy Electric Mfg Co
Chicago, Ill :......... Sperry Electric Co
Peoria, Ill :.............Royal Electric Co
Rockford, Ill :........ Rockford Electric Mfg Co
Fort Wayne, Ind :...Fort Wayne Electric Co
Indianapolis, Ind :...The C. D. Jenney Co
Terre Haute, Ind :...Kester Electric Co
Davenport, Iowa :...Hawkeye Electric Mfg Co
Boston Mass;........ Consolidated Electric Mfg Co
Economic Electric Mfg Co
Kimball F. M., & Co
Thomson-Houston Electric Co
Van Choate Electric Co
Fitchburg, Mass:... Colburn J. W., & Co
Lowell, Mass:........ Eastern Light and Storage Battery Co
Detroit, Mich :........Detroit Electrical Works
Standard Electric Co
Woodward Electrical Co
St. Paul, Minn :...... The Acme Electric Co
St. Louis, Mo :........Heisler Electric Light Co
Brooklyn, N. Y :......Brooklyn Electric Construction Co
Elektron Mfg Co
Mutual Electric Mfg Co
R. & B. Electric Mfg Co
New York City :..... Anglo-Am. Electric Light Mfg Co
Ball Electric Light Co

New York City :..... The Clark Electric Comp
                     Cleveland Motor Co
                     Continental Dynamo Co
                     Daft Electric Light Co
                     Easton Electric Co
                     Electric Construction and Supply Co
                     Electric Accumulator Co
                     Empire City Electric Co
                     Eureka Electric Co
                     Excelsior Electric Co
                     Gibson Electric Co
                     Isolated Accumulator Co
                     Julien Electric Co
                     Macroon Storage Battery Co
                     New Am. Electric Arc Light Co
                     New Century Electric Co
                     Sawyer Man Electric Co
                     United Edison Mfg Co
                     U. S. Electric Lighting Co
                     Wenstrom Northern Electric Co
Cincinnati, O;........G. F. Card Mfg Co
Cincinnati, O :........Queen City Electric Co
Cleveland, O :.........The Bruch Electric Co
Lima, O :................Silvey Electric Co
Philadelphia, Pa :... Aurora Electric Co
                     Electro Dynamic Co
                     La Roche Electric Works
                     National Electric Light & Power Works
                     Novelty Electric Co
Pittsburg, Pa ;........Westinghouse Electric Co
Eau Claire, Wis:.....National Electric Mfg Co

GAS MACHINES.—(Gas Works.)

San Francisco, Cal : H. J. Dykes & Co
                     Independent Autom. Portable Gas Works
Chicago, Ill :......... Bradley Gas Machine Co
                     Fahnejehn Incandescent Gas Light
                     Gilbert & Barker Mfg Co
                     Globe Light and Heat Co
                     Mathews Gas Machine Co
Baltimore, Md ;......Lay Gas Machine Co
Boston, Mass :........ Connelly & Co
                     National Automatic Gas Machine Co
                     Rossney Gas Saving Co
                     Gilbert & Barker Mfg Co
Detroit, Mich ;........Detroit Heating and Lighting Co
Newark, N. J :........Denny Bro. & Co
                     Smith & Sayre Mfg Co

Newark, N. J : ......Tirrells Gas Machine Co
New York City :.....Connelly & Co
      Continental Gas Engine Co
      Gilbert & Barker Mfg Co
      Natural Gas Improvement Co
      Welch & Lawson
Cincinnati, O :...... The Coleman Gas Mach. Mfg Co
      The A. J. English Co
      J. G. Isham & Co
Cleveland, O :........ The Cleveland Gas Machine Co
Morristown, Pa :.....Lowe Mfg Co
Philadelphia, Pa :...Beacon Construction Co
      Consumer Gas Works
      Gas Works Construction Co
      Louisiana Construction Co
      The Pennsylvania Globe Gas Light Co
      United Gas Improvement Co

HYDRAULIC MACHINERY.

San Francisco, Cal: Dow Steam Pump Works
      W. T. Garratt & Co
San Francisco, Cal : F. Smith & Co
      Weed & Kingwell
Ausonia, Conn :... The Farrell Foundry Machine Co
Birmingham, Ala :.. Birmingham Iron Foundry
Middletown, Conn :..W. Douglas
Wilmington, Conn:..A. Gawthrop & Son
Louisville, Ky :......Ainslie, Cochran & Co
Baltimore, Md :......Thomas K. Carey & Bros
      Ernest Frank & Son
      Snowden & Cowman
Boston Mass :........Lowell Machine Shops
Brooklyn, N. Y : ...Wm. Taylor & Sons
New York City :......The Tuerk Hydraulic Power Co
      Watson & Stillman
Alliance, O :...........Morgan Engineering Co
Cincinnati O :........John McGowan Co
Cleveland O :.........Kaufholz Bros
Dayton, O :............G. J. Roberts & Co
      The Smith & Vaile Co
Salem, O :..............Silver Deming Mfg Co
Alleghany, O .... Duff Mfg Co
Philadelphia, Pa :...Arthur Falkenau
      Tinius, Olsen & Co
Pittsburg, Pa :.........Mackintosh, Hemphill & Co
      Scaife Foundry Machine Co
Providence, R. I :... Phoenix Iron Foundry
Roanoke, Va :......... Hydraulic Engine Mfg Co

MACHINERY IN GENERAL.

Special, Experimental and Model Machinery, Etc.

San Francisco, Cal : Aetna Iron Works
     Joshua Hendy Machine Works
Denver, Col :......... Hendey & Meyer Engineering Co
     Hendrie & Bolthoff Mfg Co
     Kennedy & Pierre Machinery Co
     Western Prospecting Co
Bridgeport, Conn :.. Bridgeport Machine & Tool Works
     The Bridgeport Forge Co
New London, Conn: D. E. Whiton Machine Co
Wilmington, Del :...Trump Machine Co
Chicago, Ill :......... Berlin Machine Works
     Machinist Supply Co
     Palmer Bros
     Palmyra Manfg Co
     Porter Manfg Co
     Preble Manufacturing Works
     Schrauem & Pease
Chicago, Ill : ....M. H. Walker & Co
     S. A. Woods Machine Co
Galesburg, Ill :......Industrial Works
Rockport, Ill :........Lillibridge & Erbach
     Utter Manfg Co
Springfield, Ill : .....Gillet & Hunter
Indianapolis, Ind : Chandler & Taylor Co
     Howard Machine Works
     Steel Pulley and Machine Works
Milton, Ind :.........Dorsey Machine Co
Munic, Ind :..........Munic Engine Works
New Albany, Ind : Hegewald & Co
Dubuque, Iowa :.....Novelty Iron Works
Louisville Ky :........W T. Pyne
     Union Machine Co
Baltimore, Md :.......Bartlett, Haywood & Co
     James Bates
     Thomas K. Carey & Bros
     The Ellicott Machine Co
     H. C. Larabee
     Parker & Knight
     Stephenson & Co
Boston, Mass :.........Am Tool and Machine Co
     Atlantic Works
     Julian D'este & Co
     Edson Manfg Co
     Electric Machine Co
     Hersey Brothers

Boston, Mass :........Holmes & Blanchard
Peet Valve Co
Pettee Machine Works
Riley & Gray
Webb & Watson
Waltham, Mass:.....John Stark
Westfield, Mass:...The H. B. Smith Co
Worcester, Mass:...A. Burlingam & Co
L. W. Pond Machine Co
Pratt Sumner & Co
Detroit, Mich : ....Christian Bauman
Sam F. Hodge & Co
A. Spranger & Son
Grand Rapids, Mich : F. Hartman & Co
Kalamazoo, Mich : Strait & Packard
Minneapolis, Minn : W. Cooper & Co
Kinward & Haines Manfg Co
St. Paul, Minn :.....Lee & Hoff
Wm. Roger & Co
Meridian, Miss :.....Progressive Machine Works
Kansas City, Mo :...Jordan & Leas
Witte Iron Works
St. Louis, Mo :.......Albrecht & Schellhorn
Bignall & Keeler Manfg Co
D. A. Brislin
Chouteau Manfg Co
J. A. Crossman & Co
W. Ellison & Son
Felber Machine Works
Hood & Murray Machine Works
Mielenz, Ziegler & Co
C. Moxey & Co
E. Wachter Machine Works
Westlake & Button Novelty Works Co
Omaha, Neb :.........Omaha Model Machine Works
Paxton & Vierling
Mount Holly, N. J : T. C. Alcott & Son
Davison & Driggs
Gould & Eberhardt
W. G. Greenfield & Co
Ohl & Haffner
G. E. Parker & Co
Pierre & Noble
L. Stillwell & Co
Plainfield, N. J :.....Pond Mach. Toll Co
Trenton, N. J ;......Duncan McKenzie
Albany, N Y ;........Sullivan & Ehlers
Brooklyn, N. Y ;.....Bentley & Adams

Brooklyn, N. Y : .....Brady Manfg Co
                   Kennedy & Diss
                   James W. Lyon
                   Merrill Bros
                   J. S. Simpson
                   White & Price
Buffalo, N. Y : .....Daupster Engine Works
                   Frank & Co
                   Kendall Manfg Co
                   Niagara Machine Co
                   Niagara Stamping and Tool Co
                   The J. T. Noye Manfg Co
New York City :...Chris. Abele
                   P Backus & Son
                   Ph. J. Bender & Sons
                   Benton Manfg Co
                   · J. S. Birch & Co
                   Chas. Bramberg
                   J. DeBauvais
                   Delamater, C. D. & Co.
New York City:......Eddy, George B.
                   Emmerich & Vonderlehr
                   Jackson T. A.
                   Kek & Co.
                   Lieb Machine Works
                   N. Pattern Machine & Die Co.
Rochester, N.Y. . Connell & Dengler
                   L S. Graves & Son
Troy, N. Y :.........Andams Laundry Machine Co
                   Knowlson & Kelley
                   Tolburst Machine Co
Waterford, N, Y:...Gage Machine Works
Cincinnati, O :........Wm. Barker & Co
                   Chas Berkhemer & Co
                   Bichford Drill Co
                   The Egan Co
                   Kech & Co
                   Krieger, Burkhardt & Co
                   The Laidlaw & Dunn Co
                   Lodge & Davis Machine Tool Co
                   Muller Machine Tool Co
                   Lawrence Roth
                   Sebastian May & Co
                   Straub Machinery Co
Cleveland, O :........J. Evans & Co
                   Forest City Machine Works
                   Franklin Machine Works
                   Horsburg & Scott

                              Huntington & Lunt
                              Kaufholz Bros
                              Otto Konigslow ·
                              Langenau Manufacturing Co
                              River Machine Co
                              The Variety Iron Works Co
                              Walker Manufacturing Co
Columbus, O : .... Capital City Machine Works
                              Industrial Machine Works
                              I. G. Pulling & Co
                              The P. Hayden Saddlery Hardware Co
Dayton, O :........... Buckeye Iron and Brass Works
                              Joice, Cridland & Co
                              The Smith & Vaile Co

Alleghany, Pa :..... Specialty Manufacturing Co
Philadelphia, Pa :... Belmont Machine Works
                              Bemet, Milles & Co
                              Berry & Orton Co
                              James Cardell & Co
                              Chambers Bros. & Co
                              Enterprise Quilting Machine Co
                              Gordon & Gilbert
                              Edwin Harring on, Son & Co
                              Jos. Heginbottom Machine Co
                              Lamb Machine Co
                              National Boiler and Machine Co
                              Neafie & Levy
                              Olsen, Tinius & Co
                              Pedrick & Ayer
                              Schaum & Uhlinger
                              L. Schutts & Co
                              Taws & Hartman
                              Textile Machine Co
                              Wynn & Henwood
Pittsburg, Pa :........ Bair & Gazzam
                              Best, Fox & Co
                              Butler & Gardner
                              Franz & Braun
                              McGill & Co
                              Shook. Anderson & Co
                              S. Tretheway and Co
Nashville, Tenn :... Southern Novelty Works
Dallas, Texas :...... Hetherington & Nason
Galveston, Texas :... Walsh & Cleary
Salt Lake City, Utah : Silver and Iron Works
                              Utah & Montana Machine Co
Milwaukee, Wis :... The Wilkin Manfg Co

MODEL MAKING.

San Francisco, Cal.: Coffin, Alonzo
Bridgeport, Conn.: Platt, O. S.
New Haven, Conn.: Henn, A. S. & Co.
Lambert, Geo D.
Waterbury, Conn.: Draher, J.
Chicago, Ill :...... .. Aronson, F.
Brown, H. L.
Garden City Model Works
Meunch, Rob
Union Model Works
Indianapolis, Ind: Hood, H. P.
Boston, Mass: .... Burley, John
Steers, William
St. Paul, Minn: ...Seeger, Rob
St. Louis, Mo: .... Buchanan & Co
Medart, Fred
Jersey City, N.J: .. Currier, C. & Sons
Trenton, N.J: .. Baker, William H
New York City; . Danies, Thomas
Dutcher, G. W.
Einbigler & Adler

NEWS PAPERS.

Augusta, Me: .. Maine Farmer
Lewistown Me: . Weekly Journal
Portland, Me: .. Maine State Press
Concord, N. H: . People & N. H. Patriot
Dover, N. H: .. Morning Star
Manchester, N. H: Mirror & Farmer
Battlesboro, Vt: . Vermont Phœnix
Lyndon, Vt: .. Vermont Union
Montpelier, Vt: . Argus & Patriot
Boston, Mass: .. Sunday Courier
Weekly Globe
Weekly Journal
Mass. Ploughman
New England Farmer
New England Staaten Zeitung
Pilot
Greenfield, Mass: . Gazette & Courier
New Bedford, Mass: Republican Standard
Northampton, Mass: Hampshire Gazette
Pittsfield, Mass: . Berkshire Co. Eagle
Somerville, Mass: Journal
Springfield, Mass: Weekly Republican
Weekly Union
Worcester, Mass: . Weekly Spy

```
Newport, R. I:    Mercury
Providence, R. I.  Sunday Telegram
Woonsocket, R. I : Patriot
Bridgeport, Conn : Rep. Standard
Danbury, Conn :    News
Hartford, Conn :   Conn. Catholic
                   Conn. Courant
                   Conn. Post
                   Weekly Times
New Haven, Conn : Columbian Register
                   Sunday Register
West Winsted, Conn Winsted Herald
Albany, N. Y :     Cultivator & Country Gentleman
                   Weekly Journal
                   Sunday Press
                   Weekly Times
Bath, N. Y :       Steuben Farmers Advocate
Brooklyn, N. Y :   Anzeiger
                   News
                   Review
Buffalo, N. Y :    Aurora (Germ.)
Cambridge, N. Y :  Washington County Post
Elmira, N. Y :     Husbandman
Hudson, N. Y :     Gazette
Lockport, N. Y :   Niagara Democrat
New York City :    Am. Art Journal
                   Am. Machinist
                   Weekly Baptist
                   Catholic Herald
                   Christian Advocate
                   Evening Post
                   Weekly Herald
                   Weekly News
                   Woechentliche Staatszeitung
                   Weekly Sun
                   Weekly Times
                   Weekly World
Rochester, N. Y :  Am. Rural Home
                   Weekly Democrat
                   Express
Syracuse, N. Y :   Weekly Journal
Troy, N. Y :       Weekly Press
                   Weekly Times
Utica, N. Y :      Herald, Gazette & Courier
                   Weekly Observer
                   V. Drych
Watertown, N. Y :  Reformer
Allentown, Pa. .   Friedens Bote
```

Allentown, Pa : .....Welt Bote
Bryn Mawr, Pa ; . Home News
Doylestown, Pa : . Bucks County Intelligencer
                    Democrat
Germantown, Pa : . Telegraph, (weekly)
Harrisburg, Pa : . Telegraph, [weekly]
                    Lutheran Observer
Philadelphia, Pa : . Weekly Press
                    "   Times
                    Ver. Staaten Zeitung
Pittsburg, Pa : . . Chronicle
                    Weekly Post
                    "   Telegraph
Reading, Pa : . . .   "   Eagle
West Chester, Pa : Jeffersonian
Asbury Park, N. J: Journal
Newark, N J : . . Journal Weekly
Baltimore, Md. . . American
                    Baltimorean
                    Deutsche Correspondent
                    Gazette
                    Weekly Sun
                    Telegram
Washington, D. C : Weekly Post
                    Star
Norfolk, Va : . . . Weekly Landmark
                    Virginian
Richmond, Va : . . Weekly State
                    "   Whig
Wheeling, W. Va : Deutsche Zeitung
                    Intelligencer
                    Saturday Evening Journal
Goldsboro, N. C : . Transcript-Messenger
Atlanta, Ga : . . . Weekly Constitution
                    Sunny South
Columbus, Ga : . . Weekly Times
Savannah, Ga : . .   "   News
Mobile, Ala : . . . Register
Montgomery, Ala : Weekly Adv. & Mail
Selma, Ala : . . . Southern Argus
New Orleans, La : . Weekly Deutsche Zeitung
                    Observer
                    Weekly Picayune
                    "   Times
Austin, Texas : . . Texas Capital
Dallas, Texas : . . Weekly Herald
Galveston, Texas : Weekly News
                    "   Texas Post

Houston Texas: .   "   Age
San Antonio, Texas: "   Express
                 "   Freie Presse
Waco, Texas: . . . Examiner and Patron
Little Rock, Ark.,   Weekly Arkansas Democrat
                    "   Arkansas Gazette
Frankfort Ky., . .   "   Kentucky Yeoman
Lexington, Ky., .   "   Press
Louisville, Ky.,   . Agriculturist Legal Tender
                Weekly Anzeiger
                    "   Commercial
                    "   Courier-Journal
                Farmers Home Journal
Paris, Ky., ... True Kentuckian
Chattanooga, Tenn., Weekly Times
Knoxville, Tenn., .   "   Tribune
Memphis, Tenn., .   "   Appeal
                   "   Avalanche
                   "   Public Ledger
Nashville, Tenn., .   "   American
                Banner Weekly
Cincinnatti, Ohio.,   Weekly Abendpost
                   "   Enquirer
                   "   Gazette
                   "   Volksfreund
Cleveland, Ohio., .   "   Herold
                   "   Leader
                   "   Plain Dealer
Columbus Ohio . .   "   Courier
                   "   Ohio State Journal
                   "   Westbote
Springfield, Ohio.,   Farm and Fireside
Steubenville, Ohio., Weekly Herald
Toledo, Ohio., . .   "   Blade
Indianapolis, Ind.,   Indiana Farmer
                Indiana State Journal
                Indiana State Sentinel
                Weekly News
New Albany, Ind.   Ledger Standard
Notre Dame, Ind.,   Ave Maria
Shelbyville, Ind., . Weekly Shelbyville Democrat
Terre Haute, Ind.,   Gazette
Vincennes, Ind . . Commercial Weekly
Bloomington, Ill., . Weekly Leader
                   "   Pantagraph
Champaign, Ill., . Champaign County Gazette
Chicago, Ill., . . . Deutsche Warte

Chicago, Ill., . . .	Weekly	Staats Zeitung
	"	Inter Ocean
	"	Irish Tribune
	"	Journal
	"	Katholisches Wochenblatt
	"	Neue Freie Presse
	"	News
	"	Telegraph
	"	Times
	"	Tribune
Peoria, Ill., ...	"	Democrat
	"	Transcript
Quincy, Ill., . . .	"	Herald
	"	Whig
Rockford, Ill. . . .	"	Gazette
Rock Island, Ill. .	"	Union
Springfield, Ill. . .	"	Ill. State Register
Adrian, Mich: . .	"	Times and Expositor
Detroit, Mich. . .	"	Free Press
	"	Post and Tribune
Kalamazoo, Mich. .	"	Gazette
Fon du Lac, Wis. .	"	Commonwealth
Janesville, Wis. . .	"	Gazette
Madison, Wis. . .	"	Wisconsin State Journal
Milwaukee, Wis. .	"	Wisconsin
	"	Herold (German)
	"	Sentinel
Kansas City. Mo. .	"	Mail
	"	Times
St. Louis, Mo. . .	"	Anzeiger des Westens
	"	Missouri Republican
	"	Post-Dispatch
	"	Times
	"	Westliche Post
Burlington, Iowa. .	"	Gazette
	"	Hawkeye
Davenport, Iowa. .	"	Democrat
	"	Gazette
Des Moines, Iowa.	"	Iowa Staats Anzeiger
	"	Iowa State Register
Dubuque, Iowa. .	"	Times
Iowa City, Iowa. .	"	Republican
Keokuck, Iowa. .	"	Constitution
Marshalltown, Iowa	"	Times Republican
Sioux City, Iowa. .	"	Journal
St. Paul, Minn. . .	"	Dispatch
	"	Globe
	"	Pioneer Press

Winona, Minn. . .	"	Republican

Winona, Minn. . .   "   Republican
Atkison, Kansas .   "   Patriot
Emporia, Kansas. .   "   News
Leavenworth, Kan.   "   Appeal and Tribune
Topeka, Kansas. .   "   Kansas Farmer
                       "   Commonwealth
Lincoln, Neb. . .   "   Neb. State Journal
Nebraska City, Neb   "   Press
Omaha, Neb.. . .   "   Bee
                       "   Republican
Denver, Colo. . . Colorado Farmer & Live Stock Journal.
                   Weekly Rocky Mountain News
                       "   Times
                       "   Tribune
Pueblo, Colo. . . .   "   Colo. Chieftain
Los Angeles, Cal. .   "   Herald
                       "   Express
Oakland, Cal. . . .   "   Times
Sacramento, Cal. .   "   Bee
San Francisco, Cal.   "   Alta California
                   California Farmer
                   Weekly Chronicle
                       "   Post
Portland, Oregon. .   "   Oregonian
                   Willamette Farmer

NOVELTY MANUFACTURERS.

Bridgeport, Conn. The Hatch & Holmes Mfg. Co
Waterbury, Conn. . American Pin Co
                   Novelty Mfg. Co
                   The Chapman & Armstrong Mfg. Co
Chicago, Ill. . . . Art Album Co
                   Carr E. W., & Co
                   Inventors Exchange
                   U. S. Home Mfg. Co
                   Wunder & Co
Boston, Mass. . . . . Bay State Mfg. Co
                   M. W. Carr Co
                   Novelty Brass Co
                   Henry W. Peabody Co
                   Wells Mfg. Co
Easton, Mass. . . . . N. E. Specialty Co
Leominster Mass. . Dulite Novelty Co
Newburyport, Mass.Chrolitthion Novelty Co
North Adams Mass.Novelty Mfg. Co
Worcester, Mass. . Alex. McDonald
Detroit, Mich. . . Black L., & Co
                   Eagle Mfg. Co

Detroit, Mich :......Metallic Goods Co
St. Louis, Mo. . . . . Coe Yonge & Co
Omaha, Neb. . . . . Pioneer Novelty Co
Newark N. J. . . . . Bogardus New Art Co
                     Newark Novelty Co
                     Newark Specialty Co
N. Y. . . . . Auburn Novelty Co
Brooklyn, N. R. . . Clinton Mfg. Co
New York City.. . The Am. Artistic Gold Stamping Co
                     American Pin Co
                     Arlington Novelty Co
                     Brass Goods Mfg. Co
                     Celluloid Novelty Co
                     Eureka Trick and Novelty Co
                     The H. B. Hardenburg Co
                     Harman & Straus Specialty Co
                     Inventors Mfg. Co
                     Kaufmann & Straus
                     Mnfs. Distributing Co
                     Novelty Mfg. Co
                     Rob. Sneider
                     Union Metal Novelty Co
                     C. F. Verzier
                     Homer H. Wellman
                     World Mfg. Co
Syracuse, N. Y. . . Novelty Mfg. Co
Troy, N. Y. . . . . Troy Novelty Co
Cincinnati, O. . . International Novelty Co
                     Monarch Novelty Co
                     Queen City Novelty Supply Co
Girard, Pa. . . . . Keystone Mfg. Co
Philadelphia, Pa. . A. C. Knight E Co
                     Phila. Novelty Co
                     A. Schoenhut & Co
Watsontown, Pa. . Watsontown Novelty Co
Providence, R. I. . Towel Rack & Novelty
                     Vanstone Mfg. Co
Springfield, Vt. . . Vermont Novelty Works Co
Milwaukee, Wis. . Elite Mfg. Co

PAINT AND COLOR MANUFACTURERS.

San Francisco, Cal. California Paint Co
                     Pacific Gilt Lead Works
                     Pacific Rubber Paint Co
Chicago, Ill. . . . Brainard Paint Co
                     Cary-Ogden Co
                     Chicago White Lead Co
                     Matterson Bro & Co

Chicago, Ill :.........The Sherwin-Williams Co
Baltimore, Ill :......Rubber Paint Co
          John Briggs & Co
          C. E. Folsom & Co
          Jones & Co
          The Sherwin-Williams Co
Detroit, Mich :......Detroit White Lead Co
          Penins. W. L. and Color Works
Minneapolis, Miss: W. W. Sly Paint Manfg Co
St. Paul, Minn :......Stearns Paint Manfg Co
St. Louis, Mo :........Mound City Paint and Color Co
          G. M. Nelson Paint Co
          St. Louis Paint Manfg Co
          Standard Paint Co
New York City :.....The Andrews Paint and Color Co
          Am. Mixed Paint Co
          A. B. Assbacher & Co
          Femoline Chemical Co
          Geo. N. Gardiner
          German Color Co
          Heller & Merz Co
          New York Insulating Co
          The Prince Manfg Co
          R. F. Seaman & Co
          Standard Paint Co
          S. P. Wetherill Co
Troy, N. Y :.........Troy Paint and Color Works
Cincinnati, O : ......Fav. Paint and Oil Works
Cleveland, O: ....Iron-clad Paint Co
          Thompson Manfg Co
Alleghany, Pa : .....M. B. Snydam & Co
Philadelphia, Pa :...Eureka Paint and Color Works
          N. Z Graves & Co
Pittsburg, Pa :........M. B. Snydam & Co
Chattanooga,Tenn : Southern Paint and Color Co.
Richmond, Va :......C. W. Tanner & Co

PATENT MEDICINE MANUFACTURERS.

Chicago, Ill :...........Emmett Proprietary Co
          Foley & Co
          D. Kelly & Co
          Koenig Medicine Co
          J. B. Lynas & Co
          Marshall Medicine and Chemical Co
Boston, Mass :........Ame & Co
          Bedford Chemical Co
          Dam's Remedy Co
          Flower Medical Co

Westfield, Mass:......J. W. Colton & Co
Detroit, Mich:.........Williams, Farrand & Co
Minneapolis, Minn: German Medine Co
St. Paul, Minn:......Sigler Manfg Co
Kansas City, Mo:...Benso Medicine Co
St. Louis, Mo:........Am Remedy Co
                        S. Pfeiffer Manfg Co
                        Southwestern Medicine Co
                        Wolflard Salve Manfg Co
Newark, N. J:.......B. S. Lauderdale & Co
Buffalo, N. Y:.......Powell & Plimpton
                        D. Ransom & Co
New York City:......J. P. Bush Manfg Co
                        H. Planters & Son
                        Winchester & Co
Rochester, N. Y:.....A. B Grover & Co
                        G. Hahn & Co
Troy, N. Y:...........L. Burton & Co
                        J. L. Thompson & Co
Cincinnati, O: .....Eureka Medicine Co
                        J. N. Harris & Co
                        John D. Park & Sons
Philadelphia, Pa:...Geo. W. Ellis
Providence, R. I:...Geo. A. Peckham
Fort Worth, Texas: Dashwood Medical and Chemical Co
Fond du Lac, Wis: Stiles & Givens Co

REFRIGERATOR MANUFACTURERS.

Chicago, Ill:.........Chicago Refrigerator Manfg Co
                        Jackson Refrigerator Co
                        Lorillard Refrigerator Co
                        Geo. N. Pierre & Co
                        Ridgeway Refrigerator Manfg Co
                        Thayer Portable Refrigerator Co
                        Wickes Refrigerator Co
Morris, Ill:...........Globe Refrigerator Co
Baltimore, Md:......Roloson's Dry Air Refrigerator Co
Grand Rapids, Mich: Grand Rapids Refrigerator Co
St. Louis, Mo:........ St. Louis Refrig & Wooden Gutter Co.
Buffalo, N. Y:.. .....The Ross Pat. Refrigerator Co
                        S. Gray & Co
New York City:......Belding Mfg Co
                        L. H. Mace & Co
Burlington, Vt:......Baldwin Dry Air Refrigerator Co
Philadelphia, Pa:...John P. Maher & Co
                        Ridgeway Refrigerator Co

SADDLERY, HARNESS, &C.

Louisville, Ky :...... Harbison & Gathright
Langdon-Krieger Saddlery Co
New Orleans, La :...Baker, Slos & Co
St. Louis, Mo :........P. Burns & Co
P. J. Peters Saddlery & Harness Co
Buffalo, N. Y :........ National Harness Co
New York City :......Whitman Saddle Co
Cincinnati, O :........D. S. Carrick & Co
Grossmann, Gonvion & Co

SEWING MACHINE MANUFACTURERS.

Hartford, Conn :..... Weed Sewing Machine Co
Chicago, Ill :......... Foley & Williams Mfg Co
Boston Mass :.........Reece Button Hole Machine Co
Florence, Mass :..... Florence Machine Co
New York City ......Bonnaz Embroidering Machine Co
The Florence Machine Co
Kruse Mfg Co
National Machine Co
New Home Sewing Machine Co
Rotary Sewing Machine Co
Standard Sewing Machine Co
Tracy Sewing Machine Co
Union Special Sewing Machine Co
Wheeler & Wilson Mfg Co
Wilcox & Gibb, Sewing Machines
Philadelphia, Pa : Am. Button Hole,Overseam and S. Mach. Co
Button Sewing Machine Co
Dewees Fabric Trimmer Co
Domestic Sewing Machine Co
Lamb Machine Co
Singer Mfg Co

STEAM ENGINE MANUFACTURERS.

(See also Iron Works, Machinery, etc.)
San Francisco, Cal : Atlas Iron Works
C. H. Evans & Co
Hartford, Conn :.....The Hartford Dynamic Co
New Haven, Conn :..The Norwalk Iron Works
Wilmington, Del : ...Remington Machine Co
Chicago, Ill: ....Rob. Tarrant
Boston, Mass :........Atlantic Works
Ge. K. Paul & Co
Detroit, Mich :........The Coller Steam Yacht & Engine Works
Fulton Iron & Engine Works
St. Louis, Mo :........L. M. Rumsey Mfg Co
South New Market, N. H: Swamscot Machine Co

Buffalo, N. Y :........H. G. Trout
Fishkill-on-the Hudson, N. Y : Fishkill .anding Mach. Co
Newburgh, N. Y :...William Wright
New York City :..... N. Y. Engineering Co
                    N. Y. Safety Steam Co
                    Skinner Engine Co
                    Triple Thermic Motor Co
                    Wells Engine Co
                    Westinghouse Church, Kerr & Co
Troy, N. Y :..........Knowlson & Kelley
Salem, O :.............. ....Buckeye Engine Co
Allegheny, Pa:...... Thos. Carlin's Sons
Corry, Pa :............ H. King & Sons
Philadelphia, Pa :...High Bros & Co
                    Jos. Lumley
                    M. R. Muehle
                    Neafie & Levy
Pittsburg, Pa :........Thos. Carlin's Sons
                    Combination Engine Co
                    Robinson Rea Mfg
Nashville, Tenn :.....Davidson Engine Co
Madison, Wis :........Madison Mfg Co
Milwaukee, Wis :... The Wilkin Mfg Co
Racine, Wis :.........Racine Hardware Mfg Co

STEAM HEATING.

Denver, Col :...........Hughes & Keith, Sanitary Supply Co
New Haven, Conn :..New Haven Steam Heating Co
Washington, D. C :.. Florida Steam & Hot Water Heaters
Chicago, Ill :......... The John Davis Co
                    A. A. Griffing Iron Co
                    Rice & Witacre Mfg Co
Baltimore, Md :......Bartlett, Hayward & Co
                    Wm E Wood & Co
Boston, Mass : ....L. Descalzo & Co
                    Gurney Hot Water Heater Co
                    Kohler Furnace & Steam Heating Co
                    B. F. Sturtevant
Detroit, Mich :........Detroit Radiator Co
                    A. Harvey & Son
Minneapolis, Minn: Haptun Steam Heater Co
                    Porter Steam Heater Co
St. Paul, Minn :.......Young Safety Heating Co
St. Louis, Mo :.........St. Louis Steam Heating & Ventil. Co
Omaha, Neb :.........Strang & Clark
New York City :.....Gold Car Heating Co
                    The Gaubert Mfg Co
                    Gurney Hot Water Heater Co

New York City :.....J. F. Pease Heaters
                    New York Steam Co
Syracuse, N. Y :......Pierre, Butler & Pierre Mfg Co
Reading, Pa   Reading Steam Heating & Vintel. Works
Providence R. I :.....Providence Steam Heating Co
Milwaukee, Wis :... Bayley Steam Heating Co

STEAM PUMP MANUFACTURERS.

Los Angeles, Cal: ..Dow Steam Pump Works
Chicago, Ill   Barr Pumping Engine Co
                    Nye Steam Vacuum Pump Co
Dubuque, Ia:...   .National Iron & Brass Works
Boston, Mass :........John Post, Jr. & Co
Holyoke, Mass :......Dean Steam Pump Co
St. Louis, Mo :........Henry Worthington
Omaha, Neb; ....Churchill Pump Co
Jersey City, N. J :...Maslin's Pulsator Pump
Brooklyn, N. Y......Clayton Steam Pump Works
                    Niagara Steam Pump Works
Buffalo, N. Y.........The Buffalo Steam Pump Co
New York City......Hall Steam Pump Co
                    Woodward Steam Pump Co
Canton, O..............The Canton Steam Pump Co
Cincinnati, O........ Brandford Well and Pump Co
Philadelphia, Pa.....Barr Pumping Engine Co
                    Gordon Steam Pump Co
Pittsburg, Pa........ Kay Bro. & Co
                    Pittsburg Supply Co

STOCK BROKERS.

Mobile, Ala............F. W. Miller & Co
San Francisco, Cal: A. J. Angell
                    W. Bannan & Co
                    E. Cahill & Co
                    Donovan & Weinschenk
                    A. W. Foster & Co
                    E. Gauthier & Co
                    Greene & Co
                    C. P. Harris & Co
                    C. H. Kauffman
                    Ives & Co
                    Kuhl, Roemer & Co
                    Manheim, Staples & Co
                    H. H. Noble & Co
                    Oris & Co
                    Rehfisb & Co
                    Salomon Manfg Co
                    H. B. Smith, Jr.

San Francisco, Cal : W. D. Valentine & Co
S. B. Wakefield & Co
T. Whitely & Co
Hartford, Conn......R. R. Abbe
J. B. Russell
J. G. Woodward
New Haven, Conn...Brunnell & Scranton
W. T. Hatch & Sons
Wilmington, Del....R. R. Robinson & Co
Washington, D. C...E. Brand & Co
Cooke & Co
C. T. Havener & Co
Moore & Schley
B. K. Plain Co
B. B. Williams
Atlanta, Ga............H. Castleman
J. A. Hall
E. T. Paine
The Tolleson Commission Co
Augusta, Ga........ ..J. J. Cohen
J. U. Jackson
Columbus, Ga.........J. Blackman
Johnson & Norman
Macon, Ga............G. T. Kershaw
J. W. Lockett
Savannah, Ga.........H. Blim
J. Ehlen
G. W. Lamar
L. A. Wakeman
Chicago, Ill............C. V. Banta
D. F. Baxter
A. J. Cutler
A. Durham
L. H. Freiberger
M. Straus
W. B. Wrenn
Fort Wayne Ind :...L. C. Hurm
Lafayette, Ind : .....Potter & Orth
Louisville, Ky :...... Almstedt Bros
J. T. G Galt
John Green
New Orleans, La:...H. Bier
J. L. Herwig
J. Klein & Co
H. Lange
A. J. Louis
E. Eisenhauer
Portland, Me:........J. S. Morris

Portland, Me:........A. Shurtleff
Baltimore, Md: .....R. H. Harris
                    C. L. Howell
                    Kummer & Becker
                    G. Ober
Boston, Mass:.......Adams, Blodgett & Co
                    M. R. Ballou
                    J. H. Brown
                    Chase & Barstow
                    J. E. Hall
                    F. N. Mudge
                    B. F. Tenney
                    H. Walter & Co
                    Waterman & Co
Minneapolis, Minn: G. W. Hood, Jr.
                    M. S. Lewis
St. Paul, Minn:.....Doran M. & Co., 311 Jackson
                    Levy A. M, 20 Gilfillan blk
                    Maher E. A. & Co., 307 Jackson
                    Murray, Rank & Co, 23 Nat'l G.A. bank bldg
                    Stokes S S, 333 Jackson
                    Walker & Co, 1 Gilfillan blk
Kansas City, Mo: .Abell M. B., 11 Wales bldg
                    Arnold J H., 3 James b'dg
                  Jarvis, Conklin Mortgage Tr Co, N.E. bldg
                    Wallman W. J. & Co. 12 Wales bldg
St. Louis, Mo:......H Brentano
                    J Campbell
                    Donaldson Bond and Stock Co
                    A. G. Edwards & Son
                    L. Goldman
                    Kohn & Co
                    U S. Investment Co
                    W. F. Wernse & Co
Omaha, Neb:.........Dale J., 404 Merchants Nat. Bank bldg
                    Dike A P., 310 S 15th
                    Wilson W. A, 1418 Harney
Brooklyn, N. Y:.....J. Lehrenkrauss
                    G. H. Prentiss & Co
Buffalo, N. Y:......A. Church
                    W. R. McNiven
New York City :.....Am. Investment and Finance Co
                    G. A Bergman
                    I. S. Bernheimer
                    Blum & St. Goar
                    James Boys Co
                    C H. Currie
                    J. R. Day

New York City :...Emerson & Co
L. S. Frankenheimer
Gregory, Ballou & Co
G. M. Hahn·
Keilholz Bros
Kohn, Popper & Co
E. L Oppenheimer & Co
Randall & Wierum
Rosenheim & Herzog
1. Sonnenberger
Springer & Co ·
Rochester, N. Y :...W. C. Fox & Co
J. M. Lux
A. Robinson
Troy, N. Y : ....L. Boardman
Neher & Carpenter
Ogden, Calder & Co
W. W. Willard
Cincinnati, O :........W. S. Brown
R. E. Dunlap
G. W. Durrell
J. W. Haley
S B Keys
E. N. Laralde
I. N. Stoeckle
J. H. Vornholz
I. Wolf
Cleveland, O :........H. C. Dening
T. A. Kelley
C. H. Potter & Co
C. C. Viall & Co
Columbus, O :........Hanson & Co
J. N. Champion
Dayton, O:............M. Schaefer
J. A. Schieble
Springfield, O :......W. 8. Thomas & Bro.
L S. Weaber
Philadelphia, Pa :...H. F. Bachman
H Borden & Co
W. Curtiss
A. D. & W. P. Fell
E. Henderson
Howard, Bell & Co
F. Huth
E. W. Keene
T. C. Knight
K. W. Magill & Co
Moelling & Autenreith

Philadelphia, Pa:...W. S. Myers & Co
     E. B. Pail
     Philadeldhia Stock Exchange
     Stahl & Straub
     S. H. Thomas
     J. K. Wildman
     E. K. Wohlgamuth
Pittsburg, Pa:........S. Arnold
     S. W. Black & Co
     J. W. Drape & Co
     Geo. B. Hill & Co
     Kuhn Bros
     S. J. Pentecost
     Whitney & Stephenson
Providence, R. I: B. B. Barrows
     H. C. Cranston
     H. Pearce
     S. Frash & Co
     Q. R. Weeden & Co
     J. Wilbur & Co
Charleston, S. C:...Cochran & Alexander
     H. DeLeon
Norfolk, Va:.........Morris & Morris
     C. T. Sydner
Richmond, Va:......C. W. Branch & Co
     Davenport & Co
     R. W. Maury
     W. G. Taylor & Co
     J. C. Williams
Nashville, Tenn:...Arrington & Farrar
     J. Davis
     H. Scovel
     Moore & Co
Brownsville, Tex: E. C. Forto
Corsicana, Tex:.....Frost & Barry
Dallas, Tex: ....A. W. Childress
Galveston, Tex:.....B. A. Isaacs & Co
Houston, Tex: ......Canon & Seligson
Milwaukee, Wis:...E. H. Goodrich
     F. S. Iole
     Alexander Cohen

STOVE MANUFACTURERS.

San Francisco, Cal : San Francisco Stove Works
Denver, Col:.........Great Western Stove Co
Stamford, Conn:.....Stamford Foundry
Chicago, Ill :.........Calorific Wonder Co
     Chicago Stove Works

Chicago, Ill:.........Fuller & Warren Co
Louisville, Ky:......Bridgford & Co
                     The Progressive Stove Works
Baltimore, Md:......The B. C. Bibb Stove Co
                     S. B. Sexton & Son
                     Isaac A. Sheppard & Co
                     Wm. E. Wood & Co
Boston, Mass;   Barstow Stove Co
                     Boston Furnace Co
                     Smith & Anthony Stove Co
Detroit, Mich:......Detroit Stove Works
                     Michigan Stove Works
                     Peninsular Stove Co
Minneapolis, Minn: Northwestern Stove Works
St. Paul, Minn: .....Central Stove Works
Kansas, Mo:.........C. W. Fairman Stove Co
St. Louis, Mo:........Bridge & Beach Co
                     Evers Stove Mfg Co
Omaha, Neb: Duffey Trowbridge Stove Mfg Co
Albany, N. Y:......Albany Stove Co
New York City......J. L. Mott Iron Works
                     Peekskill Stove Works
                     Richardson & Boynton Co
                     The Richardson & Morgan Co
Rochester, N. Y:...Sill Stove Works
Troy, N. Y;.........Troy Arch. Iron Works and Foundry
Cincinnati, O: ......Chamberlain Stove Co
Cleveland, O:........Winslow Safety Car Stove Co
                     The Standard Lighting Co
Columbus, O: ....Capital City Stove Co. Works
Mansfield, O: ....The Ohio Valley Foundry Co
Philadelphia, Pa:...Abraham Cox Stove Co
Pittsburg, Pa :........Crea, Graham & Co
Nashville, Tenn;..Phillips & Buttorff Mfg Co
Milwaukee, Wis;...Brand Stove Co

TINWARE MANUFACTURERS.

Chicago, Ill:.........Chicago Stamping Co
                     Chicago Tin & Hardware Co
                     C. Shepard, Sidney & Co
Baltimore, Md:......Mathews, Ingram & Co
Boston, Mass:........Dover Stamping Co
                     Lalaurge Grosjean Mfg Co
                     Hollander, Bradshaw & Folsom
Elmira, N. Y:........S. H. Laney
New York City......The Central Stamping Co
                     Reilley Bros
Cincinnati, O: ......The Cincinnati Stamping Co

Cincinnati, O: ......Western Tin and Japan Mfg Co
Philadelphia, Pa:...C. P. Pool & Co
Milwaukee, Wis:... Kieckhefer Bros. & Co

TOOL MANUFACTURERS.

San Francisco, Cal: San Francisco Tool Co
Hartford, Conn:.....The Billings & Spencer Co
Chicago, Ill: ....Cleveland Twist Drill Co
Bangor, Me: ....E. Mansfield & Co
Boston, Mass: ....Am. Axe and Tool Co
                  Goodnow & Wightman
                  H. H. Harvey
                  Tremont Mfg Co
Springfield, Mass:.. Hardware & Tool Co
Detroit, Mich: ......Detr. Edge & Tool Works
St. Louis, Mo:........Western Forge and Tool Works
Buffalo, N. Y:......American Bit Brace Co.
New York, N. Y:...American Pneumatic Tool Co
                  American Tool Co
                  Manhattan Tool Co
Syracuse, N. Y:......Syracuse Twist Drill Co
Cleveland, O:.........Standard Tool Co
                  The Worden Tool Co
Meadville, Pa:......Barret Vice and Tool Co.
Philadelphia, Pa:..Geo. J. Ellis & Sons
                  Palmer, Cunningham & Co
Pittsburg, Pa:........Iron City Tool Works
Madison, Wis:.......Lake City Tool Co

TOY MANUFACTURERS.

Birmingham, Conn:A. B. Ruggles
Bridgeport, Conn:..Ives, Blakeslee & Co
                  C. Ritchel
                  Watson Iron Works Co
Chatham, Conn:.....Thewall Mfg Co
Derby, Conn:.........Gilbert & Sons
Durham, Conn:......Merriam Mfg Co
East Hampton, Conn: Bevis Bro. Mfg Co
                  East Hampton Bell Co
New Haven, Conn: C. D. Goodwin
Middletown, Conn: W. F. Chapman & Co
                  Samuel Kirby
Plymouth, Conn:...Whistle Wheel Toy Co
South Norwalk, Conn: Lockwood Mfg Co
Chicago, Ill:......... Chicago Toy & Fancy Goods Co
                  Colby Toy Mfg Co
                  St. Nicholas Mfg Co
Baltimore, Md:.......N. Y. Toy & Novelty Mfg Co

Fitchburg, Mass:....Novelty Turning Co
Leominster, Mass,. The W. S. Reed Co
Lowell, Mass.........Merrimack Croquet Co
New Bedford, Mass., Weedon Mfg Co
Springfield, Mass.,..Milton Bradley Co
Worcester, Mass., Rowson Bee Hive Co
Coldwater, Mich.,..Stevens & Sperry
Detroit, Mich........Henry C. Hart Mfg Co
Grand Rapids, Mich., Crescent Mfg Co
Pattersville, Mich.,....Benton Mfg Co
Bristol, N. H............A. Hutchinson
Clearmount, N. H....Union Toy Foundry Works
Nashua, N. H..........Nashua Novelty Works
New York, N. Y.,....Eureka Trick & Novelty Works
                    McLaughlin Brothers
                    The Stobel & Wilken Co
                    Weston Toy Co
                    Wilson Brothers
Cincinnati, O.,......P. J. Marqua Co
Philadelphia, Pa.,..S. E. Clark
                    James Fallows & Sons
                    D. Highman & Sons
Milwaukee, Wis.,..Instructive Toy Co

TURNERS.

San Francisco, Cal: San Francisco Wood and Ivory Works
New Haven, Con:.. The J. Smith Co
Chicago, Ill: ....M. Garrison.
                    Keller & Co
Fitchburg, Mass:....Novelty Turning Co
Worcester, Mass:...O. B. Rawson
Newark, N. J:......John B. Oelkers
Patterson, N. J:......B. Atkinson
New York City:......E. B. Estes & Son
                    New York Pattern Mach. and Die. Co
Alleghany, Pa:.......Alleg. Geomet. Wood Carving Co

VENTILATORS.

San Francisco, Cal: P. H. Jackson & Co
Chicago, Ill: ....Andrews & Johnson
                    Cool Air Drying and Ventilating Co
Boston, Mass., ...National Ventilation Co
                    B. F. Sturtevant
                    U. S. Aerophor Air Moist & Venti. Co
                    U. S. Ventilation Co
Minneapolis, Minn., Emery Mfg Co
St. Paul, Minn,......Exhaust Ventilator Co

New York City......Gouge Heating & Ventilating Co
The Simmonds Mfg Co
Standard Ventilating Co
The Sanitary Ventilating Co

WASHING MACHINES, WRINGERS, &c.

Chicago, Ill:......... Colby Wringer Co
Troy Laundry Machine Co
Fort Wayne, Ind....Horton Mfg Co
Boston, Mass.,........J. F. Baldwin & Co
New York City,..... Cataract Washing Machine Co
Empire Laundry Machine Co
The A. M. Dolph Co
Troy, N. Y..........Adams Laundry Machine Co
Cincinnati, O., ...F. M. Watkins
Alleghany, Pa........Loyal Mfg Co
Philadelphia, Pa.....Restein Mfg. Co